Forever in Love with Jesus

Discover Eight Portraits of Jesus from the Books of Hosea and John

A Bible Study by

**Dee Brestin &
Kathy Troccoli**

Thomas Nelson
Since 1798

NASHVILLE   DALLAS   MEXICO CITY   RIO DE JANEIRO

Published in Nashville, TN by Thomas Nelson. Thomas Nelson is a registered trademark of Thomas Nelson, Inc.

Thomas Nelson, Inc. titles may be purchased in bulk for educational, business, fundraising, or sales promotional use. For information, please email SpecialMarkets@ThomasNelson.com.

Unless otherwise indicated, Scripture quotations are from the New King James Version (NKJV), © 1979, 1980, 1982 Thomas Nelson, Inc., Publishers. Used by permission. All rights reserved.

Other Scripture references are from the following sources: The Holy Bible, New International Version (NIV). © 1973, 1978, 1984, International Bible Society. Used by permission of Zondervan Bible Publishers; The Message (MSG), © 1993. Used by permission of NavPress Publishing Group; J. B. Phillips: The New Testament in Modern English, Revised Edition (PHILLIPS). © J. B. Phillips 1958, 1960, 1972. Used by permission of Macmillan Publishing Co., Inc.

ISBN-13: 978-0-8499-6446-6 (repack)

Library of Congress Cataloging-in-Publication Data

Brestin, Dee, 1944–
    Forever in love with Jesus / Dee Brestin & Kathy Troccoli.
        p. cm.
    Includes bibliographical references.
    ISBN-13: 978-0-8499-1825-4
1. Jesus Christ—Person and offices—Biblical teaching.   2. Bible. N.T. John—Religious aspects—Christianity.   3. Bible. O.T. Hosea—Religious aspects—Christianity.   4. Christian women—Religious life.   5. Love–Religious aspects—Christianity.   I. Troccoli, Kathy.   II. Title.

BT203.B74   2004
232'.8—dc22   2004018611

Printed in the United States of America
12 13 14 15 16 QG 5 4 3 2 1

We dedicate this to STEVE BRESTIN,
a friend of God

Contents

Acknowledgments

We are thankful to the following individuals:

MATT BAUGHER:
*If you look up diplomacy in the dictionary,
you will find your name there.*

SALLY BRESTIN AND MARTIN FRENCH:
*Beauty and truth are woven so powerfully together
in your artistic portrayals of Christ.*

STEVE BRESTIN:
Just what the doctor ordered: rich in prayer and rich in courage.

WILLIE AAMES AND HIS TEAM AT OUTPOST:
*Who better to video a Bible series than Bibleman?
What energy and creativity!*

JILL WOLFORD JOHNSON:
Our Ruth. God can't help but delight in your servant heart.

MARY HOLLINGSWORTH AND HOLLY HALVERSON:
Editing needs crediting. It's truly an art, and you both are so gifted.

DEBBIE WICKWIRE AND DAVID MOBERG:
*We have been allowed to give our best. You've listened well.
You've freed us to fly.*

Forever
in Love
WITH JESUS

TURN YOUR EYES
UPON JESUS

"Of course He's not safe—but He's good."

Aslan II
Artist: Sally Brestin (www.sallybrestin.com)

Both the children were looking up into the Lion's face as he spoke

these words. And all at once (they never knew exactly how it hap-

pened) the face seemed to be a tossing sea of gold in which they were

floating, and such a sweetness and power rolled about them and over

them and entered them that they felt they had never really been

happy or wise or good, or even alive and awake, before.

THE CHRONICLES OF NARNIA
—C. S. LEWIS

1

Turn Your Eyes upon Jesus

*I*magine that you are going with us and a few of our friends to one of our favorite museums: the Metropolitan Museum of Art in New York City. When we arrive and get our tickets, the woman at the information booth tells us: "We have two exciting exhibits on loan from Israel. If you walk to the left, you will find portraits of Jesus from the gallery of John the apostle, who wrote so much in the New Testament: the Gospel, three letters, and the book of Revelation." Audible exclamations rise from our group, and we know we will all be going into this exhibit.

But then the woman says, "And if you walk to the right, you will find portraits of Jesus from the gallery of Hosea—the Old Testament prophet." We are kind of surprised; we look at each other: *What? Christ in Hosea? That book is filled with infidelity, prostitution, and oppression.* But we are certainly intrigued.

3

We decide to split up and meet at the Roof Garden Café for lunch. One group goes to the left, to John's gallery, the other to the right, to Hosea's gallery. Later, over chicken salads and Cokes, we talk enthusiastically about our morning.

> "My favorite in Hosea's gallery was *The Bridegroom*. Did you see His face? It was so full of love . . ."

> "Wow! I was just going to comment on *The Bridegroom* in John's gallery. Just seeing Him on that white horse reminded me of Mel Gibson in *Braveheart*."

> "Oh—after we finish eating, I want to go there."

> "The one I'll never forget from John's gallery was *The Lion of Judah*: the mane was gleaming in the sun, and the eyes seemed to penetrate with an all-knowing look."

> "That's amazing. There was a lion stalking by the side of the road in Hosea's gallery! Only he was so frightening."

As our conversation continues, it is obvious to us that the same portraits are in *both* galleries. And then, like a slow and widening light, we realize *why* there is a connection between the two. They painted the same Jesus because:

> Jesus Christ is the same yesterday and today and forever.
> —Hebrews 13:8

We had no idea when we began to write *Forever in Love with Jesus* what lay around the corner for us. We sensed a magnificent staircase spiraling ahead, but God gave us only enough light for a step at a time. Now, when we look back, we can identify with the lyrics from that famous old spiritual:

Sometimes it causes me to tremble, tremble, tremble . . .

Theologians have a term for this: the *mysterium tremendum,* or simply "awful mystery." It is the kind of encounter with God that makes your blood run icy cold. For though God is completely good and loving, He is also holy and just, and when you suddenly realize He is truly present, as close as your very breath, a part of you cannot help but tremble.

(*Dee*) One of the portraits of Jesus we will study in depth is *The Lion,* who appears in both Hosea and John. As we were writing about *The Lion,* my daughter Sally, who is a professional artist, was commissioned by a couple to paint Aslan, the lion who is a Christ figure in The Chronicles of Narnia, the classic children's series by C. S. Lewis. Sally was inspired by the following conversation that occured when the children in the story first heard about Aslan:

"Is he a man?" asked Lucy.

"Aslan a man!" said Mr. Beaver sternly. "Certainly not. I tell you he is the King of the wood and the son of the great Emperor-Beyond-the-Sea. Don't you know who is the King of Beasts? Aslan is a lion—the lion, the great Lion!"

". . . Then he isn't safe?" said Lucy.

"Safe?" said Mr. Beaver, " . . . who said anything about safe? . . . 'Course he isn't safe. But he's good. He's the King, I tell you."[1]

Each morning, before Sally began painting, she prayed that the Spirit of God would take over and flow through her. She wanted to portray both the love of Aslan and the *mysterium tremendum*, the side of Aslan that "isn't safe." Like Jesus, Aslan is wonderful because he is completely good, loving, and merciful. Yet he also "isn't safe" in that he is holy, just, and powerful. The White Witch of Narnia and all her evil could not stand against Aslan's power—nor can anyone who persists in rebellion against Jesus. There are also times when, for reasons we cannot fathom now, an omnipotent God may allow Satan or the sin in this world to pour pain and sorrow into our lives.

When Sally completed the painting, she told me she felt the "not safe" side of Aslan had emerged in it, but she wasn't sure she could see the "wonderful side." The morning after she finished, she put it on display at church. A woman came up behind Sally, and placing her hand on Sally's shoulder, said: "I love that tender lamb in your painting."

What lamb? Sally thought. She has often said that people show her different things they see in her abstract pieces—unclear images that don't mean anything to her. But when Sally walked over to the painting, the lamb was as clear as the lion. It was unmistakable.

Sally had truly not intended to paint that lamb, but she had prayed continually that the Spirit of God would work through her. When creating the lion's wild mane, she put the enormous canvas on the floor and threw down dark textures for the shadows. Then, as the paint began to dry, she removed some of it with pallet knives, making sweeping arcs to create highlights. In the process, somehow, mysteriously, a distinct lamb emerged. Not only that, he was at the lion's heart, and he looked as if he had been slain.

When the Spirit of God gave the apostle John a vision of Jesus Christ and the last days, John recorded what he saw:

Then one of the elders said to me, "Do not weep! See, the Lion of the tribe of Judah, the Root of David, has triumphed. He is able to open the scroll and its seven seals." Then I saw a Lamb, looking as if it had been slain, standing in the center of the throne.

—Revelation 5:5–6 NIV

When we first saw the lamb, we felt a chill running up and down our spines, for we knew we were in the presence of a holy God.

What we did not know, but of course He did, is that the very day Sally delivered her painting to the couple who had commissioned it, she would learn that her dad had advanced colon cancer. The doctors have not given us much hope, but we have hope, because we belong to a God who can and does heal. Though we know we cannot insist, we are crying out for mercy, as He has taught us to do.

As we walk through the deepest valley of our lives right now and realize that our fifty-nine-year-old husband and father, this godly, precious man, may be taken from us, Jesus feels like the Lion in our lives, tearing apart what we hold most dear. He certainly is not safe. Yet at His heart—and this we must always remember—is the Lamb who has been slain. When I saw the lamb in Sally's painting, I wept. For whatever awaits us with Steve's cancer, I know that the Lamb of God is at the heart of the Lion of Judah. Jesus is good, He is loving, and if I ever doubt it, I have only to remember that He died for me. The fact that His Spirit led Sally to paint this lamb without her even realizing it is just another evidence of His care, His love, and His mystery.

It is also an evidence of His care that He led Kathy and me to look at portraits of Jesus—to "turn our eyes upon Jesus." At first, we were torn between Hosea and John. Initially, when we began to plan this book, I had told Kathy I had a longing to encourage women to look into Hosea. Kathy loved Hosea as well, and in some ways, it seemed perfect for *Forever in Love with Jesus*. It is in Hosea where the Lord says:

> I will betroth you to me forever.
> —HOSEA 2:19 NIV

Yet, we knew how difficult and how dark much of the book of Hosea is. *How many would really want to study Hosea? we wondered. After all, along with beautiful metaphors of God's redeeming love are frightening descriptions of His judgment. There are many times when He is the Lion who is not safe. Are women going to be turned off before they understand what we're trying to convey?*

So we withdrew from Hosea. We began to think, *Perhaps we should study the portraits of Jesus that John paints. How encouraging it would be to study the great "I AMs" in John's gospel. Everyone would be blessed by portraits such as "I AM the Light of the World," "I AM the Good Shepherd . . ."*

Yet, still, we felt pulled toward Hosea. Which way was God leading? I went to sleep one night, praying, *Lord, I want to hear from You. It's so hard to wait. Unless You have a better idea, could You show me soon?*

I have found that if I am willing to wait on Him, as hard as that is, He does come. One night I awoke with a thought:

> Could it be that the pictures we so love of Jesus from John are also in Hosea?

I could hardly wait to get out of bed and go downstairs to where my Bible was. I curled up in my green leather chair and opened to Hosea again.

There, in the middle of the night, His Holy Spirit caused me to see portraits that had always been there but now were unveiled. We talk about "a kiss from the King," when the Word of God jumps out at us, giving us exactly what we need. I certainly was being "kissed" that night. I could identify with the two disciples who were on the road to Emmaus when a "stranger" (the resurrected Christ) joined them. Eventually, Jesus opened their eyes and showed them, "beginning at Moses and all the Prophets," pictures of Himself. (Luke 24:27 NIV, emphasis added). Over and over again, I saw the portraits John painted of *The Redeemer* and *The Bridegroom*; I also saw *The Lion of Judah*, and *The Resurrection and the Life*—there they were—in Hosea! I could hardly wait to talk to Kathy. *Please, Lord, if this is of You, put this same desire in her. Let her confirm it.*

When I explained to Kathy the parallels between John and Hosea, her eyes widened. She said, "You're right, Dee. Jesus is all over the book of Hosea. I love how tenderly devoted Hosea was to his bride, and yet there were times when he loved her with a very tough love. It is such a parallel to how God loves His church, His bride. And I think women will also understand the personal application—like in Ephesians—of 'how wide and long and high and deep is the love of Christ.' I definitely think we need to explore that. It will be exciting!"

We both have a great love for beautiful art. Seeing the parallels of Jesus in these particular books, our enthusiasm grew as we thought of portraying them visually. The visual helps us see the truth as well as hear it. In this book we will behold many portraits, as if we were wandering into a church filled with stained-glass windows. Like flickering candles, the Scriptures allow us to see the detail in these windows. Sometimes you will see a gentle Jesus, as mild as a lamb. Sometimes you will see His righteous wrath, as ferocious as a lion. What is also amazing is that you will see His tenderness and His fierce holiness within *each* of the portraits.

R. C. Sproul talks about "the trauma of holiness," the *mysterium tremendum*. When Isaiah had a vision of the holiness of God, "Every fiber in his body was trembling . . . Relentless guilt screamed from every pore." Sproul says, "It is one thing to fall victim to the flood or fall prey to cancer; *it is another thing to fall into the hands of the living God.*"[2]

> *I saw the Lord sitting on a throne, high and lifted up, and the*
> *train of His robe filled the temple. Above it stood seraphim;*
> *each one had six wings: with two he covered his face, with two*
> *he covered his feet, and with two he flew. And one cried to*
> *another and said:*
>> *"Holy, holy, holy is the LORD of hosts;*
>> *The whole earth is full of His glory!"*
> *And the posts of the door were shaken by the voice of him who*
> *cried out, and the house was filled with smoke.*
>> —ISAIAH 6:1–4

We would have been frightened, frozen—flattened! Isaiah surely was:

> *Woe is me, for I am undone!*
> *Because I am a man of unclean lips,*
> *And I dwell in the midst of a people of unclean lips;*
> *For my eyes have seen the King,*
> *The LORD of hosts.*
>> —ISAIAH 6:5

The "unsafe side" of God. We have each experienced it: *(Dee)* I was on my knees when I first received Christ into my heart, and I, like Isaiah, had a glimpse of the holiness of God and fear overwhelmed me with its icy grip. I saw my depravity, and I *knew* I deserved God's wrath. But then, as in Isaiah's case, grace relieved my fears.

(Kathy) I had just heard the doctor's diagnosis for my dear, young mother: "Six months to a year," he said. I lay weeping on a pew in the

hospital chapel, longing for God to come tenderly, to comfort me, to reassure me that He would rescue us. Like a child without a parent, I was thinking, *You've left me all alone. How could You do this to me? How could You let this happen?* In the midst of my despair, He asked me a penetrating question:

Am I not still God?

How could I ignore the voice of Almighty God? I had known Him long enough to recognize that He is the Creator, the Lord of lords, the Holy One. How could I *dare* not answer His question?

How vital to see that the "unsafe" side of God is only and always meant for our good, to cause us to trust Him, to repent, to return, and to run into His arms. When we do that, He fills our hearts with singing, and we go out glorifying Him.

WHEN I FALL IN LOVE

Some of you have been with us for one or both of the first two studies in this series: *Falling in Love with Jesus* and *Living in Love with Jesus*. But if you haven't done either of the other studies, it will help you to know that there are often three stages in our love relationship with Jesus:

First Love (the euphoric courtship and honeymoon time)

Wilderness Love (the painful time of questioning and doubting your Bridegroom)

Invincible Love (the deep, abiding confidence that your Bridegroom will do all things well in His time)

This land of Invincible Love could also be called:

Forever in Love with Jesus

Although you hope the honeymoon will never end, and you'd love to go straight into the land of Invincible Love, you will see in each of these portraits that Jesus may lead you into the wilderness. While you are there, it's easy to wonder what He is doing. You may walk away from Him, feeling forsaken. But those are the very times you need to keep as close to His heart as possible. That may look different for each of us, but the Bible says, "Draw near to God and He will draw near to you" (James 4:8). You will find that He will come, He'll speak tenderly to you, and He will help you to trust His heart.

Some of you may be asking at this point: How do you really draw near to God? How do you go deeper in your relationship with Jesus?

DRAW ME NEARER

We're always looking to go deeper in relationships, especially as women. When we get together, we *thrive* on intimacy:

"Tell me everything!"

"What did she say? What did you say?"

"How did you feel when that happened?"

"Did he really hear you? Did he get it?"

We don't want to linger long discussing the weather. We want to move to subjects that touch the heart—we want to confide, console, and connect. Men may be perplexed by the fact that a good cry with other women may mean for us a good day! And being with women of depth, women whose hearts and minds are filled with God, is as refreshing as sitting beside streams of water.

In the same way, if you have entered into this study, we know you want to go deeper in your relationship with Jesus, for He is the source of "living water." The sweetest times in our lives come from closeness to Him, experiencing a joy that the world cannot ever imagine. Jesus offers us this promise:

> I came so they can have real and eternal life, more and better life than they ever dreamed of.
>
> —JOHN 10:10 MSG

(*Kathy*) I love this version of this verse. So many Christian women yearn, not only for what it means to love Jesus and be loved by Him, but to experience life to the full, and have *more life and a better life than they ever dreamed of*. What does that really mean?

Recently I was speaking at a women's event and said, very tongue in cheek:

> I have lived a fairy-tale existence since I have come to know Jesus in a personal way. My life has been perfect: no pain, no problems. My prayers are always answered. God has taken away all my sinful yearnings.

I expected a big outburst of laughter, because it was *so* ridiculous—but instead, women stared at me in silence. They leaned forward in their chairs to see what was coming next. I could almost hear their thoughts:

Did Kathy find it?

Did she discover the secret?

Wow. Someone is really living it.

They actually believed someone was living a fairy-tale existence. They knew it could *never* be them, but perhaps it could be someone else. They didn't even see how preposterous my statements were because they went into La-La Land.

Why? Because we *yearn* for more. We *yearn* for deeper. We *yearn* for the happy ending. And while a land without pain and death is not available to us until heaven, a life of abundance in our souls, a richness in our spirits is available to us right now:

> *Never far from death, yet here we are alive, always "going through it" yet never "going under." We know sorrow, yet our joy is inextinguishable. We have "nothing to bless ourselves with" yet we bless many others with true riches. We are penniless, and yet in reality we have everything worth having.*
>
> —2 CORINTHIANS 6:9–10 PHILLIPS

Sometimes this kind of abundance can seem beyond our grasp. There are so many frustrations on this earth, not only because of pain and death all around us, but because we each have a bent toward sin and a frailty in conquering that bent. Repeatedly, we quench His Spirit. We think, *Will I ever conquer my laziness, my temper, my bad eating habits, my tendency to worry, or my tendency to gossip? Will I ever stop moving into the shadows, thinking I can move away from the Lord who sees everything? Will I ever stop doubting His heart when I go through difficulties?* I have tasted the goodness of the Lord, but will it ever be my true daily bread?

The last couple of years my heart has truly been opened to realize how much more God wants for me—far beyond the point of my salvation. Jesus is the Door, but we can't stop there. Paul wrote,

> Eye has not seen, nor ear heard,
> Nor have entered into the heart of man
> The things which God has prepared for those who love Him.
>
> —1 CORINTHIANS 2:9

You may wonder:

> Is that for everyone but me?
>
> How do I enter into what God has prepared for me?
>
> How do I get to this stage?

There is a simple but profound secret.

JOYFUL, JOYFUL, WE ADORE THEE

Henry van Dyke wrote lyrics to Beethoven's Ninth Symphony, creating one of the most beloved hymns in all of Christendom. It's as if God gave him a sneak peek into what brings riches to the soul.

> Joyful, joyful, we adore Thee, God of glory, Lord of love;
> Hearts unfold like flowers before Thee, opening to the sun above.
> Melt the clouds of sin and sadness, drive the dark of doubt away;
> Giver of immortal gladness, fill us with the light of day.

Do you see it? A transformation takes place in those who spend time before Him, adoring Him, *beholding Him*. His light, like the light of the sun, kills the mold and fungus that grows so rapidly in the dark, defeating us, holding us captive. His light truly "melts the clouds of sin and sadness." A simple yet profound truth—one to help you become the woman you long to be.

Have you ever thought: *How can I ever be what God wants me to be? I am so weak! I try, but I fail, time and time again.* Sanctification (the process of becoming holy) is similar to salvation (being forgiven and becoming His child). In salvation, all you had to do, basically, was look to Jesus. Many think, *That's far too simple.* But it is the truth. We are unable to save ourselves. In the same way, we are unable to become holy in our own strength. But as we look at Jesus, learning more about His character, we trust and love Him more. As we do that, we become like Him. "Beholding is a way of becoming," explains John Piper, translating 2 Corinthians 3:18 as follows:

> We all, with unveiled face, beholding the glory of the Lord, are being changed into his likeness from one degree of glory to another.

"To see God," Piper continues, "is to be changed by Him."[3] When Moses came down from the mountain after seeing the Lord, his face was shining. In the same way, those who behold Jesus are radiant.

Because of our natural pride, we can easily embrace the error of thinking we can live the Christian life in our own strength. We believe this even though we know we can't save ourselves. If we just read three chapters in the Bible each day, pray pretty regularly, go to church, and *will* ourselves to overcome the sin in our lives—then, we think, we'll get there. The problem is that the focus is on us, when it must be on God. So why is it that beholding Jesus transforms us?

Let's consider a practical example. Think about an area in which you are prone to stumble: anger, gluttony, gossip—you know what it is. You've tried and tried, yet it trips you up again and again. You know many of the promises that go with choosing the high road. Jesus tells you that He will fill you with joy and peace; that He will set you free. Yet somehow, when faced with a choice, you still often take the low road. How can simply beholding Jesus strengthen you to take the high road? It's a mystery, but here are a few of the reasons we see that beholding *is* becoming.

First, as you focus on Jesus and get to know Him better, you cannot help but love and trust Him more. Slowly, you find that when faced with that temptation, you are more likely to *believe* His promises and do as Moses did. He refused the passing pleasures of sin because, by faith, he looked forward to his reward (see Hebrews 11:25). We need *faith* in Jesus and His Word to pass up sin. The reason we choose sin is that we don't really believe that the high road is the best road. But if you grow in your realization of the wonder and power of Jesus, you are much less likely to be deceived. It's like that game children play of falling back into someone's arms. Will he catch you? When the catcher is Jesus, you can be sure He will.

Second, when you see Jesus as the holy God He is, you are humbled. When you repent, His grace comes flooding in. A biblical example is Isaiah. Transformation occurred when he "saw the Lord seated on a throne, high and exalted, and the train of his robe filled the temple" (Isaiah 6:1 NIV).

First Isaiah *beheld* God and felt desperation, crying: "Woe is me!"

Then God, in grace, touched him.

Transformed, Isaiah cried: "Here am I, send me!" (See Isaiah 6:5–8)

In the same way, when you see the holy side of God, as Isaiah did, and as you will in each of these portraits, you will naturally cry, "Woe is me!" The Lord is near to those who are broken over their sin, for He is abounding in mercy. His grace will come to you.

The secret, therefore, as simple as it sounds, is in the beholding, for beholding is a way of becoming.

We encourage you to consider the two other tools that accompany this book: the workbook and the video. We hope this book will be either an introduction or an augmentation to the workbook, as there is something about digging out the truths for yourself and discussing them with other believers that penetrates your heart in a way a book alone cannot do. The DVD gives God a chance to pierce your heart with music, art, and exhortation. Willie Aames, (*Bibleman, Eight is Enough*) has made this the most creative and beautiful Bible study video we have ever seen—and it's very affordable. But this book is a great jumping-off point.

We've looked briefly at *The Lion.* We'd like to give you just a glimpse of one more portrait, to give you a hunger and anticipation for what lies ahead.

THE BRIDEGROOM

John wrote about a bridegroom in both his gospel and the book of Revelation. We read about a bridegroom, as well, in Hosea.

Kathy and I love the metaphors, the word pictures, in Hosea. So often our love for the Lord is like the morning mist, fading even before the sun comes up. But His love for us is like that of Hosea's love for his unfaithful wife: steadfast and eternal. In case you don't know the story, Hosea's wife, Gomer, completely humiliated him by running after other lovers, who had in turn betrayed her and made her a slave. Then they were done with her and were selling her, naked, on the auction block. You would think Hosea would have been disgusted with her and walked the other way.

But to her amazement, she saw him walking boldly through the crowd of bidders. She lowered her eyes, for she was ashamed. Then she heard his voice, bidding loudly for her.

Can it be? Why would he take me back?

Then she heard the auctioneer say, "Sold!" Though Gomer felt shame, Hosea's eyes were filled with acceptance and love.

He couldn't possibly still want me.

Then she felt his soft cloak being wrapped around her, covering her nakedness.

(Kathy) This story always makes me want to weep. I know I'm not the only one who has felt that way. One of my favorite books is Francine Rivers's *Redeeming Love,* a historical fiction account of Hosea. Sometimes as I'm working in my office, I'll glance at my bookshelf, and just seeing the binding of this treasure, I am warmed and comforted. I am sweetly reminded of the unfailing love that her main character, Michael Hosea, possessed for his unfaithful bride, Angel. I probably could still find some tear stains on the pages; I identified with Angel, for I was so amazed and broken by Hosea's powerful devotion.

She hurt.
He loved.

She retreated.
He loved.

She betrayed.
He loved.

He loved and then he loved some more.

I felt sad when I came to the end of the book, because I fell more deeply in love with Michael with each chapter. When I went to bed that night, I had a strange, lonely feeling. I kept asking myself, *What is wrong with you?* I realized I had been comforted in the last couple of days by the presence of Michael—and I missed him. And then I realized, *I have Him . . . Jesus.* How easily I forget. I closed my eyes, knowing that I was loved not by a fictional hero, but by a forever *Bridegroom.*

Forever. If you have truly been drawn by Christ and have put your trust in Him, He will never leave you or forsake you. Yet there will be times when He leads you into the wilderness. In Hosea, the bridegroom was betrayed, for his bride kept running off with false lovers, so there came a point where he decided:

> *Therefore, I am now going to allure her;*
> *I will lead her into the desert*
> *and speak tenderly to her.*
>
> —Hosea 2:14 NIV

What does the desert look like? It may mean loss and pain. Jesus may allow us to feel the consequences of our sins, or He may knock away the props we have been leaning on: places, positions, or people. We may lose our savings or our health. But His purpose is never for evil, but always for good—never to abandon us, but always to draw us near. In the desert, when we are desperate, He *will* speak tenderly to us. And then, one day, He says,

> *There I will give her back her vineyards,*
>   *And will make the Valley of Achor a door of hope.*
>   *There she will sing as in the days of her youth.*
>
> —HOSEA 2:15 NIV

He will turn our "Valley of Achor," or as Kathy likes to call it, our "Valley of Ache," into a door of hope.

Let us begin.

THE GREAT
I AM

The Great I AM
Artist: Martin French (www.martinfrench.com)

He comes as the Door, He comes as the Resurrection, He comes as the Light, He comes as the Way, and the Truth, and the Life, He comes as the Good Shepherd, He comes as the Vine. He is the One who before Abraham was, is.

—R. C. Sproul

2

The Great I AM

In each of our lives, the woman who told us about Jesus said, "Read the gospel of John."

(*Kathy*) I was twenty and working at a summer office job when I encountered a girl named Cindy. She read her Bible every day at her lunch hour. One day she got out her yellow highlighter and began putting *marks* in her Bible. You've got to understand—I grew up in a home where the Bible was as big as Texas and sat on an end table. You would *dust* it, but you would never *read* it, and you certainly wouldn't *write* in it. As I watched Cindy making huge yellow marks in the Holy Bible, I said under my breath:

"Well, she may be religious, but she's going straight to hell."

Yet I knew this girl had something that I didn't. She had a confidence and a hope that were foreign to me. At the end of the summer, after I had asked her many questions, she handed me a New Testament and said, "Why don't you read the gospel of John? I'll show you where it is."

(Dee) I was a young wife when my sister Sally arrived for the weekend, full of excitement because of her new relationship with Jesus. She asked me, "Who do you think He is?"

"I don't know," I answered. "Maybe a teacher, maybe a prophet. Does it really matter?"

"Oh, it matters," said Sally. "Do you know who the Bible says He is?" Then she followed me around the apartment, reading to me from the gospel of John. When she left, I thought, *Is it true? Is Jesus really God? I don't want to give my life to Him if He is a fairy tale.* Sally had left behind a paraphrase of the New Testament with a bookmark in John.

Kathy and I devoured the gospel of John. We were both surprised and delighted at all He said He was and all He had promised. Through that great apostle, we each came to faith and repentance. What is it about John's gospel that sets it apart from the synoptic Gospels of Matthew, Mark, and Luke?

HEAVEN CAME DOWN

In this book, we will often quote Dr. Darrell L. Bock, esteemed professor at Dallas Theological Seminary and expert on the Gospels. If you can afford only one commentary on the Gospels, we recommend Dr. Bock's *Jesus According to Scripture.*

Dr. Bock says that John's gospel is different from the other three, for "John tells Jesus' story very much from heaven down."[1] Matthew, Mark, and Luke have told us where Jesus was born, how He grew up, what He did while He was on earth—the external facts. But John's gospel is different. There are no greetings, no genealogies, and no gradual explanations leading up to the true identity of Jesus. When the curtain is raised, instead of soft lights and music, we face a full orchestra, sending tingles up and down our spines:

> In the beginning was the Word,
> and the Word was with God,
> and the Word was God.
> —John 1:1 NIV

God chose John to write "a spiritual gospel," giving us pictures of Jesus as God incarnate. John's gospel reflects "a Christology of the highest order."[2] Consider the eight great "I AMs" of John, each one a claim to deity.

I AM the Light of the World. (John 9:5)

I AM the Bread of Life. (6:48)

I AM the Door. (10:9)

I AM the Good Shepherd. (10:14)

I AM the Resurrection and the Life. (11:25)

I AM the Way, the Truth, and the Life. (14:6)

I AM the Vine. (15:1)

Before Abraham was, I AM. (8:58)

(*Kathy*) As I've gotten to know Dee, I have appreciated her spiritual gifting of proclaiming the truth. She gets so excited about the treasures in God's Word, and God has enabled her to make them clear to others. She's constantly processing the writings of Charles Spurgeon, R. C. Sproul, C. S. Lewis . . . (I, on the other hand, have just finished Dr. Seuss's *Green Eggs and Ham*.) I have watched her continually wrestle with the things she reads. She often questions, "What is this passage really saying? What is God's intention here?"

Sometimes she drives me a little crazy with nitpicking through the Bible. Who cares how many cubits were in the basement of the ark? But I have to admit that in her zeal to know the truth, Dee discovers things that many of the rest of us miss. And then she gets so excited.

When we're working together, sometimes she jumps up and starts pacing, going on and on about something that might at first seem dry to me, but then I get it. So often her insights on a passage ignite my passion to know God better, and I find that first-love excitement rekindled in my heart.

Sometimes when she picks me up at the airport in Lincoln (never would I have imagined that I would be making so many trips to the cornfields of Nebraska), she starts right in with some deep theological concept. I'm thinking, *Dee, give me a break here! I've had a long trip. Couldn't we just get a little lunch and talk about something where we don't have to think quite so hard?* But she's so enthusiastic I hate to burst her bubble.

It happened again when she got into the "I AMs." We were standing at the baggage claim, and she said:

"Kathy, *The Great I AM* is in Hosea too! I was stunned when I saw it—I even called a Hebrew professor at Dallas Theological Seminary when I discovered it and said, 'Is this true? Am I seeing what I think

I am seeing in Hosea 2?' And Kath—it's there! Let me show you . . ."

And there, in the middle of the crowd pressing in to grab bags from the carousel, Dee was flipping open her big black Bible and reading to me from Hosea.

(*Dee*) Working with each other has stretched us both—but in a really good way. After I've shared something with Kathy and am overjoyed at the treasures of God's Word, I close my Bible and think:

Well, there you have it.

The truth.

That's it!

Sometimes she gets that glazed look, but sometimes—and these are the moments I love—she jumps up and says, "Dee, open that up again!" (This also happens when she takes the "plain and simple" truth and applies it to my humanness. It always starts with questions. And she's really close to my face . . .)

It happened when I was listing the "I AMs" in John to her. This was our conversation:

"Kath, there are eight of them. Some people don't count 'Before Abraham was, I AM,' because the grammatical structure is different. But I agree with R. C. Sproul that you've got to count it. It's the most important one. There aren't seven—there are definitely eight in John."

"Oh, Dee—there are so many more than eight."

"No, Kath. There are just eight."

"I can think of dozens more."

"What? No, Kath. Don't add to Scripture."

"I'm not adding to Scripture! It's just that when I apply this to myself, He's so much more than eight."

"I don't get it."

Then Kathy looked at me with the childlikeness I have come to love and said,

"When my father and then my mother died of cancer, He showed me, 'I AM Father and Mother to you.' In the areas in which I still struggle with chains, He says, 'I AM your Redeemer.' When I battled with depression and bulimia, He said, 'I AM your Deliverer.' As I sometimes struggle with my singleness, He says, 'I AM your Bridegroom.' So many times He has completed the sentence with exactly what I needed and continues to be the Great I AM in everything I need."

"Wow, Kathy. That's beautiful."

"Stick with me, Dee."

How often we've thanked God for our friendship, for helping us to see so much more together than either of us could have alone. We know that is the beauty of the body of Christ, helping one another to see, helping one another to draw nearer to the Great I AM.

WE ARE STANDING ON HOLY GROUND

The portrait of *The Great I AM* did not begin in John, and not even in Hosea, but much earlier: in the book of Exodus, the very first time a man asked God, "What is Your name?"

Moses had one of those mysterium tremendum experiences. There is a parallel to Isaiah's experience, in that the beholding led to transformation.

It was an ordinary day and Moses was out in the desert tending the flock of his father-in-law. Suddenly "the Angel of the LORD appeared to him in a flame of fire from the midst of a bush" (Exodus 3:2). Then he heard his name:

> *"Moses, Moses!" And he said, "Here I am."*
> *Then He said, "Do not draw near this place. Take your*

*sandals off your feet, for the place where you stand is holy
ground."*

—EXODUS 3:4–5

Moses hid his face, for he was afraid. In the presence of a holy
God, Moses realized his desperation. And then God said something
that should touch the heart of every one of us who is oppressed,
every one who is suffering, and every one who wonders if God sees.

> *I have surely seen the oppression of My people who are in
> Egypt, and have heard their cry because of their taskmasters,
> for I know their sorrows.*

—EXODUS 3:7

Then the Lord said,

> *I will send you to Pharaoh that you may bring My people, the
> children of Israel, out of Egypt.*

—EXODUS 3:10

Moses was immediately stammering:

> *Who am I that I should go to Pharaoh, and that I should bring
> the children of Israel out of Egypt?*

—EXODUS 3:11

And God said—and this is one of the first important concepts of
the portrait of *The Great I AM:*

> *I will certainly be with you.*

—EXODUS 3:12

Moses asked,

> *Indeed, when I come to the children of Israel and say to* them,
> *"The God of your fathers has sent me to you," and they say to*
> *me, "What is His name?" what shall I say to them?*
>
> —EXODUS 3:13

Look carefully at God's answer:

> *And God said to Moses, "I AM WHO I AM." And He said,*
> *"Thus you shall say to the children of Israel, 'I AM has sent me*
> *to you.'"*
>
> —EXODUS 3:14

The Lord cannot be compared to anyone or anything. He can compare Himself only to Himself, so He said, "I AM WHO I AM." This name is a clear declaration of deity.

The eight "I AMs" in John are the exact same words as in Exodus—literally, *ego eimi.* (This is Greek. The reason we know it is the same in Exodus as in John is because there is a venerable Greek translation of the Hebrew Old Testament called the Septuagint.) Both of these words mean "I AM," so, though it sounds odd, Jesus is saying: "I AM, I AM." This is the same repetition that Moses heard when the Lord said, "I AM WHO I AM." If you look at the reaction of both the friends and enemies of Jesus to these eight bold "I AMs" in John, you will see they knew *exactly* what He was saying. What was He saying? "I AM God." This is the prevailing theme of John. W. Hall Harris writes:

John's theology consistently drives toward the conclusion

that Jesus, the incarnate Word, is just as much God as God the Father.[3]

Let's consider just two of the "I AMs" in John. They both occur in the eighth chapter.

I AM THE LIGHT OF THE WORLD

In the opening of John, we read that "in Him was life, and the life was the light of men" (1:4). This little baby, born in a manger, was the Light of the World. Jesus Himself made this proclamation when He was a man.

The scribes and Pharisees brought to Jesus a woman caught in adultery. Right away, as women we feel incensed, for obviously, if she was *caught* in adultery, a man was there too. This double standard shows the depravity of man. But it was never a standard of God. It is very possible that this scene is a fulfillment of a prophecy of Hosea when He said,

> I will not punish your daughters when they commit
>   harlotry,
> Nor your brides when they commit adultery;
> For the men themselves go apart with harlots.
> —HOSEA 4:14

The Pharisees were harsh with this woman, saying,

> Now Moses, in the law, commanded us that such should be stoned. But what do You say?
> —JOHN 8:5

Jesus would not punish her. Instead He said,

> *He who is without sin among you, let him throw a stone at her first.*
>
> —JOHN 8:7

Convicted by their consciences, they left, one by one, until Jesus was alone with the woman. We can imagine her trembling, ashamed, and frightened.

> *"Woman, where are those accusers of yours? Has no one condemned you?"*
>
> *She said, "No one, Lord." And Jesus said to her, "Neither do I condemn you; go and sin no more."*
>
> *Then Jesus spoke to them again, saying, "[I AM] the light of the world. He who follows Me shall not walk in darkness, but have the light of life."*
>
> —JOHN 8:10–12[4]

Who has the authority to set sinners free? God alone. Then Jesus sealed this act of deity with a pronouncement of deity:

> *[I AM] the light of the world.*

God alone is light, God alone forgives sinners, and God alone is the Great I AM.

This is immediately followed by another "I AM" pronouncement, the one that caused the Pharisees to want to stone Him!

By that time the anger of the Pharisees was seething, and they argued with Jesus that they knew better than He because they were Abraham's descendants. They thought they were "in" with God because Abraham was their forefather, just the way some people think they are "in" with God because their parents are strong Christians. But Jesus refuted the Pharisees and told them that Abraham rejoiced to see the day when Jesus would come to earth. They were so angry, they scoffed and said,

> *You are not fifty years old, and have You seen Abraham?*
> —JOHN 8:57

And Jesus answered them:

> *Most assuredly, I say to you, before Abraham was, I AM.*
> —JOHN 8:58

Not "before Abraham was, I WAS," but "before Abraham was, I AM." R. C. Sproul says,

> This is one of the purest unvarnished declarations of deity that Jesus ever makes during His ministry, and it was not missed by His audience because they took up stones to throw at Him . . . They couldn't take His life, but they wanted to take His life at that very moment because they heard in His claim a claim to deity. The Eternal One who comes to this world, He comes as the Door, He comes as the Resurrection, He comes as the Light, He comes as the

Way, and the Truth, and the Life, He comes as the Good Shepherd, He comes as the Vine. He is the One who before Abraham was, is.[5]

The Great I AM to You

Before we tell you about *The Great I AM* in Hosea's gallery, we'd like you to see how personal the I AM is to you. All of us need the Lord to be the Great I AM in so many ways: in salvation, in the deep valleys of life, but also simply in everyday life.

(*Dee*) Kathy shared with me the challenges and fears she had in building her home. There were so many decisions she had to make, so many questions she had to answer: *These contractors can be a little intimidating. Who will help me? How will I do this all by myself?* As we looked at the Great I AM, she realized that Jesus was truly present with her in every step of building her home. I told her, "I think it would be great to share this. It will make the 'I AM' live for women in their daily lives."

When we actually started writing, I decided to show my prayer group the opening chapters in which this story occurred. One day, one of them said:

"I loved these chapters. There was just one part I was hesitant about."

"What?"

"It was the part about Kathy building her house."

Another nodded. "Yes—I don't think it should go in."

"Why not?"

"How many women can identify with buying a whole room of furniture at once?"

Another said, "Most women don't have that kind of money."

I objected, "But Kathy's house isn't pretentious. It's lovely, but it certainly isn't out of bounds. And she's so thankful for it, seeing it as God's provision for her. She's on the road so much and needs the refuge. I really believe God provided this for her so she could be refreshed, enjoy friends, and use the artistic gifting God gave her for interior design."

"Yes, but we don't think most women will understand."

So when Kathy came to work on the book, I told her about that conversation and the group's reservations. I suggested we take that part out of the book.

(Kathy) I was a little taken aback by what Dee told me. Quite honestly, it hurt. Something that was so new and precious—something that was such a gift from God—seemed to me was being viewed as arrogant and materialistic. Those women didn't know me, yet I realized how often we all jump to conclusions based on our own life circumstances or experiences.

When I was on one of my trips to see Dee, she asked me to go out to dinner with these women. She was excited for me to meet her prayer team, and I was just as excited to meet some of the women who were close to her. Of course, their comments were on my mind as we exchanged our hellos and started to order. I knew I had to wait a little while before I brought it up.

Finally I could wait no longer:

"I hear you don't think I should write about my new house.

There was an embarrassed silence. But then one woman said, "Well, we didn't exactly think you shouldn't write about the house. We just thought some women wouldn't be able to identify with having the kind of home that has underground sprinklers."

"If I didn't have underground sprinklers, everything would be dead by the time I came back from a road trip."

They laughed.

"You know, I understand your concerns, but let me ask you this: how many of you are mothers?"

All of them were.

"I have been at so many luncheons, dinners, and get-togethers where *all* anyone talked about was children, grandchildren, or husbands. Sometimes I do feel out of the loop—and sometimes it does seem so glaring that I don't have those things. But that doesn't mean they shouldn't share them. I want to have the kind of heart that celebrates with them. So, how would you feel if I told you not to talk about your children because a lot of women who have not been blessed with children wouldn't be able to identify?"

They were silent but nodded and intently listened.

(Dee) I'm so thankful my friends are teachable and gracious. I know they realized that night that Jesus is the Great I AM to us in different ways. For some, He will say, *"I AM the Giver of your artistic talent"*; for some, *"I AM the Provider of your house"*; and for others, *"I AM the One who gave you children."* We need to rejoice in the different ways He is the Great I AM to us. If we were honest, some of us would say, "Lord, I'm not only disappointed, I'm angry. I see You giving to so many different people in so many different ways. But can't You give this one thing to me?"

That night Kathy shared with my friends an experience she had as a little girl. When she was done, their eyes were filled with wonder. Their attitude had changed.

One said, "You've got to put that in the book *before* you tell about building the house. It will help women understand so much about you—but also about themselves."

Another said, "And it shifts the focus completely to God and His graciousness. How He made us in a certain way and, because He knows our frame, also knows exactly how to delight us."

I STAND IN AWE OF YOU

(*Kathy*) I was in second grade, and we were going on a field trip. I would have loved to be going to the New York planetarium or the Museum of Natural History. Those were exciting, not only because of what we'd see, but because they were in New York City. But there we were, piling on a bus, going to a home of a president. I had in my heart that it was probably going to be pretty boring, but at least I wasn't going to be stuck in a classroom.

My mother was along as a teacher's helper because my mother was *always* along. She was Brownie leader, Girl Scout leader, cafeteria aide, and catechism teacher—not because she necessarily liked doing any of these things, but because she felt she was the very best one to watch over us.

We drove onto an estate lined by majestic trees and landscaped gardens. There stood a twenty-three-room Victorian structure overlooking Oyster Bay Harbor and Long Island Sound. It was called Sagamore Hill, home of President Theodore Roosevelt. It served as his summer White House. There I was, a wide-eyed little girl walking into this house that had velvet ropes across the doorway of every room. It didn't take me too long to realize that though I couldn't step into the room, I could step into the memory of it.

Something immediately happened in me. I was totally taken by the surroundings: the high ceilings, the intricate craftsmanship in the heavy furniture, the solid silver candelabras, the white porcelain tubs with claw feet, the wood floors that creaked (even the sound warmed my soul), and the smell of "old." (There was an abundance of wood—mahogany, black walnut—and all kinds of worn leather and velvet. There were books, quilts, and paintings. How could there not be an aroma of life?)

What made the scene come alive for me even more was that the staff had set up the rooms so it seemed as though the family was still living there: spectacles on the desk, a cane leaning against the door, shoes by the bed, and dinner on the dining room table. It was fascinating to see how high and yet how small the beds were. How could a little Italian girl from New York even conceive of having to step on wooden steps to get into bed at night?

As I was pondering that, the tour guide said, "As a matter of fact, this is where President Theodore Roosevelt breathed his last breath." I remember just staring at the bed. All sorts of emotions ran through me. That little twist in my gut at the realization that everyone will die. And yet, even though he was dead, and his family was no longer alive, it was almost as if they were gone for the day and were coming back. I kept thinking, *These windows have seen so much. These floors have felt so much. The walls have heard so much.* Little did I know that that moment would make me fall in love with antiques and all the charm of that era. It all survived and had a story to tell.

We piled into the bus at the end of the day, and everyone immediately started chatting. (You can picture a bus full of second graders: even after a long day, though tired, they're still rambunctious.) In contrast, I sat quietly next to my mother and stared out the window with such a sorrow in my heart. Leaving Sagamore Hill was like leaving a friend. I couldn't have articulated it at seven, but it was the beauty, and romance, and simple joy of old-time America that ignited my heart.

My mood was pretty obvious, so my mom asked me what was

wrong. All I could do was cry. I'm sure she thought something was desperately wrong, but little did we know, because I was far too young to express it, that a yearning for truly experiencing the passions of life was being awakened. I laid my head on her lap and sobbed.

Poor Mom. How do you console a child who is crying, not out of hurt but out of that deep part that has been designed to feel, and be aware, and breathe in all the riches of God's creation? When God knit me together in my mother's womb, He made me an artist. This has nothing to do with me, but it has everything to do with my Creator and how He blessed me. He gave me, even as a little girl, eyes to see, and a longing to create beauty.

SANCTUARY

How sweet of God to give me a home of my own, a place that was the fulfillment of a little girl's dream: a place that would reflect His beauty, His peace, and His goodness. I look at it now and am filled with gratitude. As I said before, when I began to build this home in Nashville, I knew I would have to face many challenges. What did I know about shingles, sprinklers, and siding? With every question, I almost heard Him whisper:

> *How will I build this home on my own?*
>   *I AM your Provider.*
>
> *There are so many choices. Which one is right?*
>   *I AM your Counselor.*
>
> *I feel so alone in this.*
>   *I AM your Companion.*

I *love* that He is my Companion. I had no idea that within a month, I would affectionately refer to my home as "a house of belonging." I named her Gracie. I've been keenly aware of the comfort of His presence. I belong there, and I belong to Him.

For years I had envisioned my own home, buying magazines such as *Architectural Digest* and *House Beautiful*, absorbing the pages with a passion. Now I was actually touching and seeing what I had held only in my imaginings. Every woman knows how it feels to picture something, whether it is a beautiful table setting or an outfit accessorized from head to toe. I had imagined the rooms that I now actually experience. I curl up in my leather chair and look up at the great room, the hub of the house. It's a grand living room with twenty-foot ceilings, a fireplace, and lots of space for me to incorporate what I've gleaned from many photographs in all of those magazines.

God knew how much, with my traveling schedule, I would need a haven. He's also put a strong desire in my heart to be surrounded by loveliness.

Because we are made in the image of God, we have a strong creative bent. Dee talks about how when we begin a book, we "hover over the face of the deep," waiting on God to turn on the light and help us bring beauty out of chaos. In the same way, when I began to visit different furniture stores, I felt a bit overwhelmed by all the furniture that wasn't at all what I wanted. Though I didn't know exactly what I was looking for, I knew I wasn't seeing it. I felt so much anticipation during the time I had saved for that moment, I surely wasn't going to blow it on things that I felt mediocre about.

I had gotten a little discouraged after a long day of "What can I help you with, ma'am?" (Don't you feel old when they call you that?) There wasn't anything they could help me with because I didn't see anything I wanted.

But in the very last store on my journey, I walked through what seemed like a giant warehouse. Suddenly my eye caught a huge chocolate leather chair with Old World markings. As I was walked toward it (I just wanted to run my hands over it), a gigantic armoire caught my eye. It was distressed ivory, and I started imagining two-foot candleholders on top and huge pieces of pottery on the shelves. As other unique pieces grabbed my attention, I began to wonder how they'd look all together. I turned around and said, "Can you help me, miss?" (I knew better than to call her "ma'am.")

I know she was expecting me to inquire about a particular piece, but instead I said, "I think I'm going to need lots of help! There are a number of items I love, but I must see them together. Can you get a couple of guys to position it all as a completed room? I promise: if I like it, I'll take it all."

Slowly they put the room together. I watched the beauty unfold. It was perfect for my house.

GIVE THANKS

Recently I had some downtime. Between my schedule and the hub-bub of moving in, I'd experienced only a day here or there in my new home. But during one particular week, I got a dose of what my soul really needed.

I had left an old guitar out on one of the chairs, delighting in the fact that friends often picked it up and strummed a chord or two. I personally hadn't played for a long time. I've liked having the talent of my guitar player and my piano player out on the road with me, and I've *loved* having long fingernails. Right then, during my off time, I didn't have any of them. So I began to play a few chords.

I felt like weeping. It hit me all over again: *Provider. Comforter.*

Companion. I guess, in the way you never forget how to ride a bike, I began playing a song that I loved hearing years ago. I don't know where he is now, but a guy named Ron Downey wrote many songs that moved my heart to tears years ago.

> When I'm with you, I'm in another world.
> Everything in life just fades away.
> With Your presence You enthrall me;
> All You've got to do is call me.
>
> With Your voice You wipe away my every tear.
> When You are near
> I just can't keep myself from falling
> Falling in love with You.[6]

(Dee) What I love about Kathy's story is how it ended up being a worship experience, for she was so aware of who had been her Great I AM. God blesses us all the time, but so often we don't recognize His hand. It's as if we move about with blinders on. An unexpected smile thrown our way, a rose sky on a summer's eve, or even just a comforting bowl of Campbell's chicken noodle soup on a cold winter night— all sweet, but we give no thanks. We're like the nine lepers whom Jesus healed. We leave joyfully but fail to acknowledge the Great I AM. God touches us with His mercy every day, but we walk around with veiled eyes and hearts, numb to the life of Christ around us.

THE GREAT *I AM* IN HOSEA

The problem with God's people in the time of Hosea was that they also were walking around with veiled eyes and hearts. He had provided so much for them, but they did not realize it or give Him thanks.

What had broken God's heart was that His people had been running to other gods, thinking *those* gods had been their provider, their comforter, and their husband. The Lord accused His bride of her infidelities with her very own words:

> For she said, "I will go after my lovers,
> Who give me my bread and my water,
> My wool and my linen,
> My oil and my drink."

—HOSEA 2:5

His people did not know who *The Great I AM* truly was.

> For she did not know
> That I gave her grain, new wine, and oil,
> And multiplied her silver and gold.

—HOSEA 2:8

So, to bring His people to their senses, the Lord said,

> Therefore I will return and take away
> My grain in its time
> And My new wine in its season,
> And will take back My wool and My linen,
> Given to cover her nakedness.

—HOSEA 2:9

It is here where we see the "unsafe" side of the Great I AM. For if He is the Light, He can certainly turn out the light. If He is the Door, He can shut the door. If He is the Bread of life, He can withhold the bread. If He can give, He can certainly take away. And He may choose to do any of these things at times. Yet His purpose is never to hurt us, but always to help us, to bring us to repentance, to restore us, to help us to become the faithful bride He longs for us to be.

A terrifying moment came in Hosea when God decided to separate from His bride for a time. This was not divorce, but separation. His purpose was not to end the relationship, for God will never do that, but to restore the relationship to what it was intended to be. For a time, the Lord told His bride,

> *I am not [your] husband.*
>
> —HOSEA 2:2 NIV

The "I AM" here is again *ego eimi*. For a time, the Lord would not be all the things a good husband can be: Protector, Provider, Counselor, and Comforter. But Hosea saw that the wedding vows would be renewed, and the Lord again would be the Great I AM to His bride.

In this scene, the bride was repentant, and three times in quick succession, the Lord said, "I will betroth you to Me."

> *I will betroth you to Me forever;*
> *Yes, I will betroth you to Me*
> *In righteousness and justice,*
> *In lovingkindness and mercy,*
> *I will betroth you to Me in faithfulness,*
> *And you shall know the LORD.*
>
> —HOSEA 2:19–20

The Lord one day will again be the Bridegroom, the Provider, the Comforter, the Great I AM. It's a fascinating passage, a passage that R. C. Sproul says laid buried in Hosea for centuries. Look at it:

> I will show my love to the one I called "Not my loved one."
> I will say to those called "Not my people," "You are my
>   ]people"; and they will say, "You are my God."
>
> —HOSEA 2:23 NIV

For a while, Sproul explains, God withdrew from Israel because of her spiritual adultery. And during that time, He grafted in the Gentiles. Because of Israel's prostitution, we who had no intrinsic claim to Him became His bride. See the fulfillment in 1 Peter:

> Once you were not a people, but now you are the people of God; once you had not received mercy, but now you have received mercy.
>
> —1 PETER 2:10 NIV

If you have put your trust in Christ, you are His bride. Once you were not one of His people, but now you are. Once you had not received mercy, but now you have. Once He was not the Great I AM to you, but now He is. How He longs for you to be, from this day forward, for better or for worse, forever in love with Him.

THE WORD

The Word
Artist: Martin French (www.martinfrench.com)

Word of the Father,

Now in flesh appearing!

O come, let us adore Him, O come, let us adore Him,

O come, let us adore Him, Christ the Lord.

—JOHN FRANCIS WADE

3

The Word

Dee) It's Christmas Eve. I am young enough that Mother is clasping my mittened hand tightly. Enormous snowflakes are falling softly, and I stick my tongue out to catch them. My older sisters are skipping on either side of Dad, who turns, his handsome face filled with joyful expectation, and flashes Mother a smile. I don't know exactly what awaits us, but the excitement is contagious.

Then the steeple appears, and then the stained-glass windows, majestically displaying their grandeur, illumined by hundreds of candles within. I try to peer inside, but all I can see are dim reflections through the glass. "O Come, All Ye Faithful" beckons angelically from organ pipes, floating out between the wooden doors, opened wide. Mother sings along softly:

Word of the Father, now in flesh appearing!
O come, let us adore Him.

It is one of my first memories of the majesty of God, of the invisible made visible through the beauty of the night, the music, and the mystery of Christmas Eve. I would be a woman before I understood, truly, who the Word of the Father, the Christ of Christmas, was.

BREATHE

The Word is a term only John uses, though the concept is throughout Scripture. There are three primary truths in this portrait of *The Word*, and understanding each can breathe life into you:

First, *The Word* is "God with us" (His supportive presence—as seen in Exodus).

Just as with the portrait of *The Great I AM*, with *The Word*, John communicated that, not only is Jesus God, but He is with us. *The Word* is John's term for the preincarnate Christ.[1] He is just as much God as God the Father (John 1:1). Therefore, Jesus has always existed, but He left His throne and became flesh in order to be with us (John 1:14). Just as the Lord Jesus, as God, was with His people in Exodus, He is with His people today.

Second, *The Word* is a communicator (His holy law—as seen in the Torah).

This term *the Word* refers both to Scripture and to Jesus, showing that God's message and God's person are inseparable. E. Stanley Jones wrote: "A great wind blew through the Bible, and lo, it stood up a Man."[2] God communicated to Moses, to Solomon, to Hosea, to John, and to all the writers of Scripture. The Author of the Torah (the Law, the first five books in the Bible), the Author of the Scriptures, and the One who communicates God to us is Jesus.

Third, *The Word* is *The Master Artist*. (His wisdom and creativity—as seen in Creation).

Jesus, in the mystery of the Trinity, created the world and all its riches. "All things were made through Him" (John 1:3). Just as He made the world out of chaos, He is making beauty out of the chaos of your life. Just as He brought to completion creation, so He who began a good work in you will bring it to completion (Philippians 1:6).

THE WORD IS "GOD WITH US"

This is, perhaps, the most critical concept, and we'd like to use three songs to unfold its truths.

"O Come, O Come, Emmanuel"

(Dee) This hymn from the ninth century always sends chills up and down my spine (and I'm thrilled to hear Kathy sing it on the video!). We often sing it early in Advent, reminding us of the longing of our ancestors before Christ:

> O come, O come, Emmanuel,
> And ransom captive Israel,
> That mourns in lonely exile here,
> Until the Son of God appear.

Emmanuel means, literally, "God with us" (Matthew 1:23). When John said, "And the Word became flesh and dwelt among us" (John 1:14), the verb "dwelt" is literally "tabernacled," or "pitched his tent." Just as He was with His people in Exodus, He came to earth, in the form of a baby, to be with us.

We as believers should celebrate the Incarnation, should celebrate Christmas with great joy, for it is the miracle of the Word, of

God Himself, coming down to dwell with us. This concept of God being with us is called the *memra,* or the supportive presence of God among His people, as seen in Exodus.[3]

When Kathy and I first started writing together, I always wanted to encourage our readers in the spiritual disciplines of prayer, reading the Bible, memorizing. . . And Kathy would say, "Dee, let's not do the 'quiet time' thing. I'd rather write about practicing His presence." I've come to see the wisdom in her thinking, for it is so easy for us in our natural depravity to reduce Christianity to a half hour in the Bible in the morning, a few rules (no swearing, no smoking, no sex outside of marriage), and going to church. Instead, the essence of God's heart is not this segmented approach but Emmanuel—"God with us." What does that look like? As honestly as we can, let's take a look at moments in a day of two desperate women (Kathy and me).

> 2:00 a.m. *(Dee)* Can't sleep. I wake, as I often do, and immediately begin to worry (about Steve's cancer, about being fat, and about things as trivial as an ugly chair I just bought). I talk to my anxious soul, reminding it of episodes of God's faithfulness in just the last day. Then I pray through Psalm 103. (I memorize because I'm desperate—if I don't pray through Scripture, my mind immediately turns back to Dee, Dee, Dee. But memorized passages help me focus on Jesus and dialogue with Him wherever I am.)

> 5:00 a.m. *(Dee)* I am up—I shower. For me, a lot of practicing the presence of God is in not seeing a separation between the physical world and the spiritual world. I enjoy the hot water and soap, the big fluffy terry towel, my soft flannel robe, my steaming mug of coffee, my fra-

grant pine candle, and my green leather chair. My heart has gratitude for all these gifts from Him. And yes, my green leather chair is where I have my quiet time. (And honestly, I have had many quiet times where I do *not* practice the presence of God. Instead I go immediately to my list of requests and read my chapters and never truly connect with God.) But today, I ask Him to be with me, sing to Him, and truly have a sense of anticipation when I read my Bible that He will "kiss" me. This is an Emmanuel quiet time, and it is so good.

9:30 a.m. *(Kathy)* I walk out my bedroom door (four and a half hours later than Dee). I turn on all the lamps in my living room. By looking out the window, I know that it's wretchedly cold out there. I'm so glad I'm still in my pajamas. I head for the kitchen for my beloved Maxwell House coffee. (Even though it's a Starbucks world, I'm still a regular-cup-of-joe kind of gal.) Making my coffee in my percolator makes me happy. (I still think that perco- lated coffee is sooooo much better than the drip kind.) As I'm going through my morning, I whisper to Him, *Jesus, thank You for this peace. After all I've been through, I never take for granted mornings like this where I'm peaceful, I have a feeling of safety in my home, and I look forward to the day. I love You, Lord.*

2:00 p.m. *(Kathy)* I am riding alone in my car on I-65 in Nashville. I have just left a long meeting and decide to check my messages at home. As I am calmly listening to them, I hear my gynecologist's voice. "Hi, Kathy. Please contact me as soon as you can. I've gotten the results of your pap smear back." Because I lost both my parents to cancer, fear and dread invade my heart—it was as if I am caught in a net for a couple of minutes and I can't get out. But then I remember to open my mouth and speak. *Jesus, whatever she says when I call her back, I put my life in Your hands. I trust You. Give me the grace for whatever comes my way. And even now, Lord, pour Your blood into every cell of my body.* Oh, the comfort to have Almighty God on my side.

3:00 p.m. *(Dee)* I make a sarcastic remark to our daughter because she mumbled instead of speaking clearly. I see the hurt in her eyes. *Why can't I just speak the truth in love? Why do I have to be mean and snipe at her? She's hurting so much already with Steve's cancer—can't I even give her the grace to mumble?* I gasp for grace the way a dying man gasps for air. I am able to ask sincerely for her forgiveness, and she gives it graciously. I seem to make the same mistakes again and again. It seems the only way I can stay in the light is to be continually confessing and repenting. *Will I ever quit? I know I won't until I see Jesus face to face. But I remind my soul that the mighty power of God is at work in me and He has made progress.*

The Word is "God with Us"—Emmanuel—the memra, or God's supportive presence with His people.

"O Come, All Ye Faithful"

(Kathy) The Word is "God with us," and part of that truth is that Jesus is God incarnate. Growing up, Dee sang "O Come, All Ye Faithful" in

her Protestant church, and I sang it in my Catholic church (John Wade, a Catholic layman, wrote the lyrics in 1743.)

So many of us have been brought up with those familiar Christmas songs. I loved to hear that first Christmas song in the mall or on the radio and realize that the time had arrived. I couldn't wait to take the Christmas stuff down from the attic. For many, many years we owned one of those metallic silver Christmas trees—you know, the kind that looks as if its needles are made out of thin pieces of tinfoil. Year after year, we got it out of the box.

Now, most of you know that seeing a wilted real evergreen tree is a sad sight, but picture a wilted tin foil tree. I loved it though. Then I couldn't wait to take out the color wheel. It had four slices of yellow, green, red, and blue plastic that rotated in front of a light bulb and made a faint constant buzzing noise. I still loved it.

I used to say, "Mom! Put on Mitch Miller. We need some Christmas music while we're decorating." I knew every single word and felt a true warmth in my heart—but boy, I sure did not know who I was singing about. The first year that I experienced Christmas as a Christian, I felt like dropping to my knees every time I heard a carol. I was overwhelmed by the good news, the true news. Jesus was real, and He was my Lord.

Many of us may associate "O Come, All Ye Faithful" with warm Christmas memories, but it was actually written, in part, to combat frequent heresies and is filled with sound doctrinal truths. The original second verse of "O Come, All Ye Faithful" has been dropped from most hymnals, but it contains the most important truth about *The Word:*

> True God of true God, Light from Light Eternal,
> Lo, He shuns not the Virgin's womb;
> Son of the Father, begotten, not created;
> O come, let us adore Him,

O come, let us adore Him,
O come, let us adore Him,
Christ, the Lord.

In this verse, John Wade made it clear that Jesus is true God of true God! He is eternal; He was not created like the rest of us, He was begotten. (The idea that Jesus was created was a heresy refuted in the Epistles and in the great creeds. Unlike us, Jesus, though He was fully man, was conceived by the Holy Spirit. Unlike us, Jesus has always existed. Unlike us, Jesus is fully God.) Wade also tapped into the important doctrine that Jesus was willing to leave His throne: He "shun[ned] not the Virgin's womb."

Another verse from this carol that is often, but not always, included is this one:

Yea, Lord, we greet Thee, born this happy morning,
Jesus, to Thee be all glory giv'n;
Word of the Father, now in flesh appearing!

Jesus is Lord, and to Him all glory should be given. The deity of Christ and His atoning work for us are the hardest truths for the modern mind. These are the truths the enemy works day and night to keep hidden from the souls of men.

People are willing to accept Jesus as a teacher, a prophet—but God? They are willing for Jesus to be one way to God, but the *only* way? They welcome Him as a moralist, but as the divine Being who died for them, that they might be forgiven? Forgiven? Of what? They might acknowledge frailty in being human, but identifying it as sin is another thing. Why would they need a Savior?

John 1:1 has often been turned and twisted, for many cannot accept what it says. Yet plainly John begins,

The Word was God.
—JOHN 1:1

(*Dee*) When my daughter Sally was nine, two members of a cult knocked on our door and she ushered them into comfortable chairs in the living room. "I'll go get my mother," she promised. She came running upstairs, whispering, "It's those people that don't understand about Jesus!" I thought, *This is certainly not what I wanted to do this morning.* Sensing my irritation, Sally said, "Mom, you told me we should show them the love of Jesus!"

Inwardly I groaned. "Pray for me," I pleaded, going down to face them. Sally ran to the kitchen, stretched out on the floor, and eavesdropped, seeing if I would indeed be nice to them. When I first told Kathy this story, we had a typical interaction:

"Dee, she let them in? I would have marched down, and although they wouldn't have overtly seen my anger, I would have said, 'I am *so* not interested. You'll need to leave now.'"

"Kath! No! I can't believe you would do that!"

"Why not? It's the truth!"

"But it's rude! I can't even imagine ushering them out."

"Sure, Dee, let your daughter bring the ax murderers right in. Serve them tea!"

"Oh Kath. This is rural Nebraska. They were young women in long dresses. No axes."

Kathy nodded, then threw up her hands. "But isn't it hard to know how to handle those situations with people knocking at your door with their agenda of bringing you the 'truth'?"

"I don't like to see them coming. It's intrusive. But the reason I had told Sally that we needed to be nice to them is because the Lord had really convicted me about my past reactions. I'll show you the passage He used." I opened my Bible and showed Kathy:

And the Lord's servant must not quarrel; instead, he must be kind to everyone, able to teach, not resentful. Those who oppose him he must gently instruct, in the hope that God will grant them repentance leading them to a knowledge of the truth, and that they will come to their senses and escape from the trap of the devil, who has taken them captive to do his will.

—2 TIMOTHY 2:24–26 NIV

"I really hear what you are saying, but Dee, should we really be asking them to come in and sit down? Should we really be 'welcoming' them?"

"Truly, it takes discernment. If you are a young Christian, you should turn them politely away. There is a strong warning about this in 2 John. Yet that should be balanced with the call to evangelism, for some young cult members may be open. Often you can find out at the door if there is any openness to the gospel: you can tell them Jesus has changed your life and ask if you can share your story.

"It is important to understand these are real people who are misguided, and we should have compassion for them. The teachings of Scripture and the model of Christ is that we should be careful, but *always* kind. It's not a sappy kindness that overlooks everything and embraces naively, but it responds with the wisdom and love of Christ. If you sense a strong resistance, it is appropriate to politely but firmly speak the truth in love. I have said things like, 'I know you have been told to be wary of those who think differently than you do. I would just ask you to cry out to God to show you His truth. If you ever have questions about what you've been taught and want to talk, please come back.'"

That day, I knew God used His Word to put compassion in my heart for these two young women. How deceived they were. How trapped. I knew if I brought up a scripture showing them the deity of Christ, I would get a knee-jerk, memorized response, for they had been trained in the lies of their leader.

So, instead of entering into a dispute over the Scriptures, I gently shared from my heart how Jesus had changed my life. Though one woman shut down, I could tell the other was really listening. After they left, I prayed with Sally that Christ's love and light would open their eyes and help them escape the chains that were holding them so tightly.

Recently I met a young girl who used to be a Jehovah's Witness. I asked her, "How did you get out?" It was interesting to me how she had really been taught to fear anyone with a different message, yet God wooed her. She heard some people talking about the study *Experiencing God,* and she went to a Christian bookstore and bought a copy, did it herself, and came to understand the true Jesus: that He *is* God, and that He died for her sins.

The biggest and most dangerous trap is the bold lie that Jesus is not God. It is the truth the cults have skewed and the truth the modern mind cannot see. How often do you hear lies like these?

"There are many ways to God."

"It doesn't matter what you believe, as long as you believe it sincerely."

"All religions are basically the same."

"It is too narrow to say Jesus is the only way."

"Jesus is a great teacher—but God?"

"Scripture doesn't really claim that Jesus is God."

Many of the cults have specialized in that last one, corrupting the many Scriptures that proclaim Christ's deity. And yet it is so clear! Consider just this one verse that we have looked at already: John 1:1. Daniel Wallace, in *Greek Grammar Beyond the Basics,* explains that the Greek construction of the phrase "and the Word was God" is the most concise way grammatically to call *The Word* "God" and yet make some distinction.[4] Jesus, in the mystery of the Trinity, is God.

Psalm 2, one of the clearest messianic psalms, talks about nations and kings who rage against God, who take counsel together against God "and His Anointed," Jesus. But the psalmist says that God "sits in the heavens" and laughs. How could anyone be so arrogant to think he could resist God Almighty? One day "His Anointed" will come on a white horse and wage war against the nations and the spiritual forces of darkness that have conspired against Him and His bride. We are to fear, "the wrath of the Lamb," John tells us, for no one who stands against His truth will prevail. On that day,

> *The kings of the earth, the princes, the generals, the rich, the mighty, and every slave and every free man hid in caves and among the rocks of the mountains. They called to the mountains and the rocks, "Fall on us and hide us from the face of him who sits on the throne and from the wrath of the Lamb! For the great day of their wrath has come, and who can stand?"*
>
> —REVELATION 6:15–17 NIV

It is interesting to hear John talk about "the wrath of the Lamb," for a lamb seems the most tender of creatures. Yet, again, even in the Lamb, we see both the "unsafe" side of Jesus, the holy and just side, and the "wonderful" side, the gentle and merciful side.

The image of a baby in a manger is a tender one, but John gives a dramatically different portrait of *The Word* in the last book of the Bible: Revelation.

> *I saw heaven standing open and there before me was a white horse, whose rider is called Faithful and True. With justice he judges and makes war. His eyes are like blazing fire, and on his head are many crowns. He has a name written on him that no one knows but he himself. He is dressed in a robe dipped in blood, and his name is the Word of God. The armies of heaven were following him, riding on white horses and dressed in fine linen, white and clean. Out of his mouth comes a sharp sword with which to strike down the nations. "He will rule them with an iron scepter." He treads the winepress of the fury of the wrath of God Almighty. On his robe and on his thigh he has this name written:*
> KING OF KINGS AND LORD OF LORDS.
> —REVELATION 19:11–16 NIV

Again, as with the Lamb and *The Lion*, Jesus is both gentle and fierce. The baby born in a manger will become a mighty Warrior.

"Battle Hymn of the Republic"

When we were little girls in public elementary school, we sang the lyrics to "Battle Hymn of the Republic." This song was inspired by the description of the scene John painted of that great and terrible day when Christ returns to do battle with the enemies who have opposed His bride.

We are very aware that "Battle Hymn of the Republic" has another meaning, for it was written during America's Civil War and implied that truth was all on the side of the North. We doubt that children sung it in elementary schools in the South, and the song may still be a source of pain to Southerners. So let us clearly say that it is shortsighted and arrogant to assume God was on the side of the North, for clearly, sin was found on both sides. (We recommend the movie *Gods and Generals* to stimulate thought and discussion about the results of this conflict.)

Today, in the long aftermath of this war, there are *still* hard feelings, and there are *still* reconciliation efforts going on in our beloved country. We certainly do not want to add to the hurts from this war, and so we prefer to think of the lyrics of this hymn only in regard to Christ's return, when surely, there can be no debate that the truth is completely on His side.

One day, the One who rested His head on Mary's breast, the One who had noplace to lay His head, the One who wore a crown of thorns, will be trampling out the grapes of wrath and loosing the lightning of His terrible swift sword. Revelation tells us He will be wearing many crowns, or diadems, woven together into one great crown, representing His complete sovereignty over all. When a king conquered an army, he wore the crown of the king of that army. Jesus one day will rule over all, for He is indeed the King of kings and Lord of lords.

We have considered the first truth:

The Word is "God with us."

The next important truth is:

The Word is a communicator.

THE WORD IS A COMMUNICATOR

Speak, Lord, in the Stillness

When *The Word* spoke the world into being in Genesis, it was Jesus, in the mystery of the Trinity, speaking the world into existence. When "the Word of the Lord came to Hosea," it was Jesus, in the mystery of the Trinity, speaking to Hosea. When the Law was given to Moses, it was Jesus communicating the heart of God to His people. Not only does the Word include the *memra,* or God's supportive presence among His people, but it contains the Law: the words, and the holy judgment of God as seen in the Torah.[5] (The Torah is the first five books of Moses: Genesis through Deuteronomy.)

This communicative aspect of the Word has both a terrible and wonderful side. It can feel terrible when it convicts us of sin. It can seem harsh when you read of someone being cast out into the outer darkness where there is weeping and gnashing of teeth. It can be wonderful when we hear how wide and high His love is, when He tells us He will never leave us, and when He promises us that one day, we will no longer weep.

Because God is always good and just, what may seem terrible is not. It is a holy mystery. The picture of Jesus coming on a white horse one day with fire in His eyes and a sword in His mouth causes us to tremble. And yet, that day is when He is waging war against all the enemies of His bride, because He is holy and just. We have come to love this picture of Jesus because we see the sword being used on our behalf and in our defense. The sword, Paul told us in Ephesians 6, represents the Word of God, and we can use it, as well, to defeat our spiritual enemies. When the enemy comes, and he will, we can use the sword of the Spirit, the Word of God, against him.

(*Dee*) As we are battling Steve's cancer, I have found that this is indeed a spiritual battle. It is as if the enemy is pushing in every window, throwing seeds of doubt, despair, and discord. I am most vulnerable to his cruel and hateful attacks in the night. As I lie awake in the dark, he begins to taunt, *How will you possibly get along without Steve?* My tears start, and soon I have to leave Steve's dear sleep-warm body and go to another room, so that my sobs will not awaken him.

One night, I e-mailed my friend Jan Silvious and said, "I am praying with my whole heart for healing, but I realize God is not obligated to heal Steve. When I think about that, I begin to sob. And then I think, *Well—but what if God has mercy and heals Steve? Then all these tears, all these sleepless nights, and all these days when I am walking about like a limp rag are in vain.*"

Jan e-mailed back with a verse that has sharpened my sword, and I am now pulling it out of my covers when the enemy comes in the night.

> *Give your entire attention to what God is doing right now, and don't get worked up about what may or may not happen tomorrow. God will help you deal with whatever hard things come up when the time comes.*
>
> —MATTHEW 6:34 MSG

Amazingly, the enemy flees into the black night with the bats where he belongs. My tears stop. And I have the energy to be the kind of wife Steve needs me to be. In this valley, I am memorizing Scripture like crazy so that I am ready for the enemy's attacks wherever I am: doing housework, in the shower, biking, or in bed. I am wielding my sword, and the enemy is fleeing.

We love the double meaning of the Word, referring both to Scripture and also to Jesus. Because God's message and His person are inseparable, it means there is great life in Scripture. Hosea compares the power of *The Word* to the spring rains and how they bring forth fruit from the earth.

He Will Come to Us Like the Spring Rains

(Dee) My business manager, Jill, is married to Keith Johnson, a farmer. Recently when she arrived at my home she looked out and saw that it had begun to rain. She let out a little cry of joy, saying, "Praise God," and walked out on the back porch. I knew what she was feeling, reveling in the steady downpour. She knows how hard her husband works every day from dawn to dusk, and she has also seen all that work wiped out by a devastating drought.

In other words, Jesus, as the Word, is here with us and is filled with wisdom, power, and comfort. And as He, through His Spirit and His Word, falls upon hearts eager to receive, He cannot help but produce fruit.[6] Hosea talked about the Lord coming to us "like the spring rains" (6:3 NIV). Likewise, Isaiah extends the analogy, and in his picture is an exciting truth:

> *For as the rain comes down, and the snow from heaven,*
> *And do not return there,*
> *But water the earth,*
> *And make it bring forth and bud,*

That it may give seed to the sower
And bread to the eater,
So shall My word be that goes forth from My mouth;
It shall not return to Me void,
But it shall accomplish what I please,
And it shall prosper in the thing for which I sent it.

—Isaiah 55:10–11

Do you see? Once rain and snow have started falling, they never suddenly reverse their course. In the same way, once *The Word* has started speaking into our hearts, it doesn't all of a sudden, like a child, say, "I take it back." Once He has started a new creative work in us, He will bring it to completion.

(*Kathy*) The Spirit has certainly been moving upon my heart, and often He has used His written Word to rain on me and bring forth fruit in my life. I've often told my friends and even my audiences that being in my forties has been a delight. My twenties were painful. My thirties were wobbly. And in my forties, I'm catching my stride a little. I love how the Lord uses years to mature us and let us live well into our stories. We truly begin to have a testimony—and our testimonies can bring healing and comfort to others because they show the faithfulness of the Lord.

I want to tell you about a time when God used the Word in my life powerfully. In 1984, I was at one of the lowest points of my life. I had a full-blown eating disorder, I was struggling in getting accustomed to the culture of Nashville (as an Italian New Yorker, I was a minority of one), and I was a national artist but a babe in Jesus. A relationship had just ended painfully. Many days were filled with tears. As a matter of fact, my roommate, Allyson, dried my eyes and put me on the plane for my next concert, when I just wanted to stay under the covers.

I remember one night going to a concert in Nashville, hoping to find some comfort and strength, but instead I ran into the one who had just broken my heart. As many of you can understand, it's an excruciating experience to encounter an ex, who still means so much to you, in a crowded room. Your thoughts go something like this: *Oh, there he is—should I ignore him? Should I go over and say hi?* All the while your stomach is churning, and you feel like throwing up.

While you are processing all of this, he is laughing, being social, and acting like you don't even exist. You may try to reach out (and I did, that night), for you know his tender side, but he treats you, not as one who is loved, not even as a dear friend, but as an irritation. After my encounter, I sat through the concert devastated, with the deepest ache in my heart. I tossed and turned that night. Yet somehow (the grace of God!), I still had the strength to go to church on that Sunday morning. I was weary, and I was drooping like a flower in need of water, but I was there. And it was there that I received the wonderful living words of God.

Brown Bannister, the producer of some of my recordings, was leading worship at my church back then. He is so talented and so gentle, and the hymns were pouring over my soul like a gentle rain. I opened to Psalm 34 while everyone was singing. Oh how I needed to hear His Word! Just then I felt as if the Lord said to me,

> I want you to get up in front of the congregation and read this psalm out loud.

How could He require that of me when I was in such a state of despair? But I knew it was God. *Lord, I can't even lift up my head, and You want me to get up in front of the church?* I kept my head down, took a deep breath, and thought, *Well . . . You'll have to give me a sign.*

Almost immediately, Brown said, ""Hey, as we're singing, let's speak God's Word to one another."

I looked up in shock. *Could it be any clearer?* Though my broken heart weighed me down, I managed to stand up. As I made my way to the altar, I kept thinking, *God, You never cease to amaze me.* I set my Bible on the podium. I remember how my hands were shaking as I turned to the psalm.

> *I will extol the LORD at all times;*
> *his praise shall always be on my lips.*
> —PSALM 34:1 NIV

I could feel the tears welling up and my throat tightening. I read:

> *This poor [woman] called, and the LORD heard [her];*
> *he saved [her] out of all [her] troubles.*
> *. . . The eyes of the LORD are on the righteous,*
> *and his ears are attentive to their cry.*
> *. . . The LORD is close to the brokenhearted*
> *and saves those who are crushed in spirit.*
> *A righteous man may have many troubles,*
> *but the LORD delivers him from them all.*
> —PSALM 34:6, 15, 17–18 NIV

I choked the words out through my tears, and I knew that I was boldly and intentionally standing on those promises. When we are going through trials, sometimes we think we'll never get out. We think we will never see the light of day, but I have found that weeping does just last for the night, and joy comes in the morning. My heart, in many areas, has been slowly and deeply mended and healed. He *has* heard me. He *does* hear me. He *will* deliver me out of my troubles.

So often we want our hearts to be instantly freed from the pain. We want the situation remedied, the relationship reconciled, and the addiction removed. But we must trust His timing and His heart on how "to deliver us out of our troubles." Just as the spring rains cause the seed to grow, so will *The Word,* but it is in His time, and in His way.

(Dee) How interesting that as Psalm 34 was "watering" Kathy in Nashville, restoring her, it was "watering" me in Seattle, restoring me. As a young woman, I was afraid to stay alone when Steve was working as a medical intern at the hospital all night. I was convinced a man with a nylon stocking pulled over his face was going to climb in my downstairs bedroom window and do terrible things to me and to our two babies. I tried to plan how I would escape, running to their cribs, grabbing one in each arm, and then climbing out their window. Could we escape? I doubted it! So I tossed and turned, paced the floor, and was exhausted the next day.

A godly older woman suggested I memorize Psalm 34 and pray back to God the promises in it. I did—and I focused on the part about "the angel of the LORD encamps all around those who fear him, and delivers them" (v. 7) One day I realized that God's promise had been fulfilled, for He had "delivered me from all my fears" (v. 4). I was sleeping peacefully. It amazes me that I have never had those kinds of fears since.

We have considered that:

1. *The Word* is "God with us" (His supportive presence—as seen in Exodus).

2. *The Word* is a communicator (His holy law—as seen in the Torah).

and next,

3. The Word is *The Master Artist* (His wisdom and creativity—as seen at Creation).

How encouraged you will be to see that just as the breath of God hovered over the face of the waters in Genesis, so the breath hovers over us. Jesus is the Master Artist, and He longs to make you a woman of beauty.

THE MASTER ARTIST

The Master Artist
Artist: Martin French (www.martinfrench.com)

O Lord, how manifold are Your works!

In wisdom You have made them all.

The earth is full of Your possessions—

This great and wide sea,

In which are innumerable teeming things.

—Psalm 104:24–25

4

The Master Artist

(Kathy) Have you ever wondered why each of us has a creative bent? We are creative because the Master Artist is creative, and He made us in His image. Some women love to create flower beds of brilliant colors. Some women love to create a dinner that tantalizes all the senses. Some women love to create a "look" and enjoy all the shopping that goes along with it. Some women are the kind of fun moms who end up having all the neighborhood kids at their houses because they dye Easter eggs with them or help them turn the basement into an Indian reservation, complete with card-table teepees and broomstick horses. I love to create an atmosphere in my home and be surrounded by beauty.

(Dee) In addition to all the other gifts God has given Kathy, He has given her an ability to create atmosphere in a home. She could be an extremely successful interior decorator! To walk into Kathy's new home in Nashville is almost a holy experience. God has given her such an eye for how to create ambiance. She's constantly humbled at the way He has provided for her in her singleness. I was at the housewarming her best friends threw for her, and as they thanked God for this provision and spoke words of life over her concerning God's faithfulness, Kathy wept. Her home has become a place of refuge for her in the midst of her hectic traveling schedule. Kathy planned it all: the colors, the rich woods, the artwork, the leather chairs. Truly, it is a sanctuary, and as she mentioned earlier, Kathy has affectionately named it Gracie.

I have always wanted a home that was a sanctuary as well, but somehow, I just don't have the "gift." I've tried by myself and even hired interior decorators, but the results have always fallen so short of my dreams. So recently, when Kathy and I were writing in my family room, I turned to her and asked, "What do you think about this new leather chair?"

(*Kathy*) I thought, *Okay, here's another chance.* I had barely touched on the look of this room a couple of times with Dee in the past and knew it was a sensitive subject. Thank God her new piece was a beautiful oak Mission chair, so I could truly compliment it. "I love this chair," I said, smiling. "It would be great to see this room go more in that direction." (Boy, was that the understatement of the year!) She nodded and said words that were music to my ears:

"I know this room is all wrong, but I can't figure out why."

Ahhhh—time for the kill. "Dee, are you open to some changes?"

"Sure."

I pounced. "Those heavy curtains have to come down."

"Really?"

"Dee, I'm so sorry, but sunlight can't even get into this room."

"I guess we could take some of them down."

"They *all* need to come down."

"Well, I guess I could take them to the Salvation Army."

"I don't think they'll even take them."

Before Dee changed her mind, Sally and I began to whip down what felt like acres of dark flowered fabric. Hauling them into the garage was an aerobic workout. When they were down, I said, "Now, Dee, I know you like flowers. I know there were flowers on the curtains. And I know you painted flowers on these white stucco walls to match all the other flowers, but it only made things worse. The walls are still hospital-like." (I couldn't wait to paint over those flowers.)

I think Dee wanted to take her marbles and go home at this point. But she hung in there with me. I was thankful for the trust.

"Are you okay to just spend a little money?"

With a childlike resignation she sighed, "Well . . . yeah."

"Where can we shop in Kearney?"

"Wal-Mart, Hobby Lobby, and Target."

I was up for the challenge. "Let's go!"

(*Dee*) Little did I know my room would be practically completed in three days. It was like an episode of *Trading Spaces*. Each day, we stopped writing at about three. I followed this wild woman at a mad pace through every available store while she pointed at lamps, picture frames, and tables and said: "This might work! Let's try that! And that! And that! Dee, if it doesn't work, we'll just take it back." I never had shopping carts piled so high. The next day, she said, "We need to go to a Home Depot."

"Sorry—no Home Depot."

"Okay. Well, just get me to a paint store."

Poor Kathy. She had a color in her mind she knew would work, but we ended up trying six different colors because of all the opinions in my house. We realized after she was done that she had a vision, and we didn't. We ended up going to the first color she picked out: a rich sage green. I will never forget Kathy's singing "Praise God from whom all blessings flow" as she painted over my flowers on the white stucco walls.

When we ventured into Kearney's furniture store, Kathy sprinted with her long coat flying behind her. She was on a mission. I watched a poor salesman try to keep up with her. She said, "We'll try this [a sofa] and this [another sofa], and come with me over here. I need this [a coffee table] and also this [a lamp]. We'll need to have them today." (It was 4:30 p.m..)

The startled salesman said, "Oh ma'am—I don't think we can still deliver today."

"Oh yes, you can," Kathy said confidently. (I was cringing in the corner.) Then she said, "There's a hundred dollars in it for you." Then she smiled sweetly, "I'm from New York, sir, that's how we do it there."

I thought, *Whose hundred dollars?*

Not only was the furniture delivered in the next half-hour, they waived the hundred dollars and were all eating right out of her hand. By the time she left, my room was transformed. It is invitingly warm, beautifully lit, and cozy yet elegant. It looks like everything I have ever wanted. People walk in and are amazed. "Ohhhhhhhhh! What happened?"

I just say, "Kathy Troccoli was here."

FOR THE BEAUTY OF THE EARTH

(Dee) One of my favorite hymns is "For the Beauty of the Earth." In fact, my precious daughter-in-law Julie, who has so many creative gifts, painted an old coffee table for me with women dancing in a meadow filled with flowers. On the sides, in calligraphy, she painted the lyrics of this lovely hymn:

> For the beauty of the earth,
> For the glory of the skies,
> For the love which from our birth,
> Over and around us lies.

When Kathy redid my family room, painting over all my flowers, she finally announced the flowery coffee table simply didn't belong in that room anymore. Before Kathy could heave it on the heap going to the Salvation Army, I rescued it. This table reminds me of my daughter-in-law's love. The hymn reminds me of God's love. Every morning the beauty of the earth is evidence of His love, and His desire to bless us, for He delights in His people. Jesus made this world for us.

When I was a young woman and my sister came to visit me, following me around with her big black Bible, it was a huge surprise to me when she said Jesus made the world. "Jesus wasn't alive then," I said, naively.

"Yes, He was," my sister said. "It says that the Word was with God in the beginning. He has always existed. Look," she said, thrusting her massive Bible under my nose. She pointed at a verse:

> *All things were made through Him, and without Him nothing was made that was made.*
>
> —JOHN 1:3

That was a lot to ponder. It still is.

Do you understand what this means for you? *The Word* that created the stars, the sunflowers, and the eagle out of nothing is at work in your life. No matter how you've blown it, no matter how little you feel you have to offer, He has the power to transform you. *The Master Artist* who used words to command beauty out of chaos in the first creation also uses His Word to bring beauty out of chaos in us.

Charles Spurgeon explains this so beautifully. Spurgeon is called "the preacher of preachers" and lived in England in the 1800s. Twice a week he preached in a sanctuary that held eight thousand (without a mike!), and people lined up for blocks in hopes of getting a seat. If we had lived then and there, we definitely would have been in that line! The eloquence, the romance, and the power behind his words existed only because God was with him. Read carefully this excerpt from a sermon delivered on a Thursday evening, January 23, 1873:

> We cannot tell how the Spirit of God brooded over that vast watery mass. It is a mystery, but it is also a fact. . . . These real facts may illustrate the work of God in the new creation. . . . The work of the Holy Spirit in the soul of man is comparable to his work in creation. . . . That same Master-Artist has drawn lines and curves of spiritual beauty upon the souls of the redeemed. . . . The very first act in the great work of the new creation is that the Spirit of God moves upon the soul as he moved upon the face of the waters . . . and where the Spirit came, the work was carried on to completion.[1]

God is at work in you, molding you, shaping you into a vessel of beauty.

We love the movies, such as *Cinderella, Sabrina,* and *My Fair Lady,* where a woman is transformed through the help of an "artist." We have a much more competent Artist at work on us who can do amazing things if only we can learn to yield to Him. In the story of Hosea, He was doing the makeover of makeovers. Gomer, Hosea's wife, was unfaithful, rebellious, and deceived. Gomer's story is our story, for Gomer not only represents God's people, but every person.

Until I Was Loved by You

Many of us have seen couples that are so mismatched, we wondered, *How did they ever get together?*

> The life-of-the-party man with the wallflower wife

> The boyfriend who never says a word and his busybody girlfriend

> The couch-potato guy and the jogger girl

You get the picture. So imagine this . . .

You are at a dinner table with several people, and there is a pastor across from you who reminds you of a young Billy Graham. He's substantial and well spoken. He's extremely wise and sensitive to the people around him.

Next to him is a woman who is obviously unsophisticated, chewing gum as she talks loudly. Her makeup is caked on in layers, and her cheap perfume dominates the table. She is wearing a very low-cut dress and leans over to talk to everyone, flirting with the men. *Who is she?* Your jaw drops as the pastor puts his hand over hers and says, "I'd like to introduce you to my *wife.*"

Perhaps this is how the Israelites reacted when Hosea introduced

Gomer. *Why would a godly prophet like Hosea marry such a blatantly promiscuous woman?*

It is in Hosea where the aspect of *the Word* as Artist is lived out in a very personal, painful, yet in the end, hopeful picture.

The Word Is a Painter of Pictures

He is a communicator, and He will use the written word but also pictures and parables to turn the light on in our minds and communicate the heart of God to us. In Hosea He painted a picture that penetrates in a way mere words could not. He commanded Hosea to live out a parable before the eyes of His people so they could understand that they, like Hosea's wife, were unfaithful brides, and that God, like Hosea, was a brokenhearted lover.

The Word Is a Potter of Clay

He is the Creator, and He will be intensely involved—skillful in and sovereign over our lives, as is a potter with his clay. He will use the water of the Word, as the potter uses water with the clay, to keep us pliable and to conform us to the image of Christ. He will take an immoral woman, like Hosea's wife, and fashion her into a vessel of honor. He is doing the same with us.

Let's consider each of these to discover what they have to do with us, and how Hosea's story exemplifies each of these actions of the Word.

OPEN THE EYES OF MY HEART, LORD

Pictures have the power to open the eyes of our hearts. The prophets often used object lessons to portray God's truth, just as in the

Gospels, Jesus used parables. Jeremiah wore a yoke around his neck, Ezekiel ate a scroll and had the haunting experience of seeing a graveyard of bones come alive. There is something about a picture that taps into our right brain in a way that mere words cannot.

Whenever we can find a painting from a great artist on a Bible narrative, we love to share it with you, because pictures add light to our understanding. Though it is important to realize that every piece of religious art is the artist's own perception of the event and must be flawed because of his human limitations, still, his perception stimulates thought, and that is healthy. It is particularly challenging to portray the Lord Jesus Christ, for no one who lives today knows what He actually looked like. In fact, there are some who say artists should *not* portray Him, and that we shouldn't have pictures of Jesus, but we don't agree.[2] When Rosalyn Cook, a gifted artist, created her first monumental sculpture of Jesus for the World Vision headquarters (a hunger relief agency), she said the enemy would come to her in the night, taunting her, saying, *Just who do you think you are to portray the Lord Jesus?* Dramatically, Rosalyn recounted her response:

> I would lie on my back in my bed and put my body in the
> shape of a cross, trying not to disturb Hal [her husband].
> I would scream into my pillow: "Greater is He who is in
> me than he that is in the world"!

Her sculpture of Jesus giving bread to children of many races is poignant and soul stirring. How thankful we are that the sword of the Spirit Rosalyn wielded sent the enemy fleeing!

When we were studying portraits of Jesus from Hosea and John, we thought it would also be wonderful to portray each of them pictorially. Could we find the specific pictures? Were they out there? And if we couldn't, could we find the right artist? So as we looked over artists, we prayed, *Lord, it would so great if You would lead us to someone who knows and loves You.*

The artist who impressed us didn't have any biblical drawings, yet still we thought he might be the one. Finally we asked him—Martin French—to try his hand at a portrait of Jesus as *The Master Artist* (the Potter.) When he sent his drawing, we were both taken by his ability to capture the heart of God. Kathy said, "Oh—he's got to know the Lord."

An accompanying letter from Martin confirmed this. It was filled with a testimony of vibrant faith, and excitement about this opportunity to portray the Jesus he so loves.

Just as actual pictures turn the light on in our minds, word pictures can bring illumination as well. Do you remember when David had committed adultery with Bathsheba? He seemed oblivious to his sin until Nathan came to him with a vivid word picture. Suddenly David *got it* and wept before the Lord in genuine repentance. Word pictures tap into emotions in a way mere words cannot. Nathan could have said, "David, it was wrong for you to commit adultery with another man's wife." Instead, Nathan used a parable that helped David understand the pain his sin had caused.

One woman told of wanting to leave her husband simply because she thought she could "do better." The friend who penetrated her heart was not the one who threw Scripture in her face but the one who painted what her life might be like in a few years. She said, "Imagine going to your child's basketball game, and your child is distracted because you and your husband are on separate ends of the bleachers. How will you feel when you look at family albums with your children and see pictures of your once-whole family?" The woman stayed in her marriage, went to counseling, and experienced a spiritual renewal and a rekindling of deep love for her husband.

(Kathy) I know that some of the most powerful songs the Lord has given me are filled with word pictures. One woman spoke to me about lying awake at night, contemplating suicide, until she heard a recording of "Hold Me While I Sleep":

HOLD ME WHILE I SLEEP

Feeling like this day has been the longest one I've known;
Time goes by so slowly when it rains.
I have carried heartache like a chain today;
I need to lay it down.
Oh the tender of surrender
When I hide in You.

Hold me when while I sleep.
Let me feel You breathe,
Your heart next to mine.
It's a taste of heaven.
Hold me while I sleep.
There I know I'm free.
In Your love I find
A peace that covers me.
Hold me when while I sleep.[3]

To tell someone that the Lord will never leave her is so true, but to paint the picture of the intimacy of being in His arms pierces so much more deeply into her aching soul. This woman said she was able to truly picture the presence of the Lord with her, and that He was, by His Spirit, holding her and comforting her in the middle of the night.

"Good-Bye for Now" is a song I wrote after Princess Diana and Mother Teresa died within days of each other. I couldn't help but think about how lonely the world felt without the presences of these two women, however different they were. I reached into my own soul for how I felt the first couple of days after both my mother and father passed away. I wanted to capture the deep loss and yet the confidence in God's promise that we will see our loved ones again through Jesus Christ. I could write a book about the reactions that I have received from thousands of people:

> "I haven't been able to cry since my mother died—today I shed my first tear in twenty years. That song released me to do so."

> "Thank you. You reminded me that I will see my husband again. The deep pain in my heart wasn't allowing me to believe it."

> "The comfort I felt today in knowing I will see my baby again brought a joy to my heart I haven't felt for a very, very long time."

GOOD-BYE FOR NOW

I can't believe that you're really gone now,
Seems like it's all just a dream
How can it be that the world will go on
When something has died within me.
Leaves will turn
My heart will burn
With colors of You.
Snow will fall

But I'll recall
Your warmth.
Summer wind
Breathing in
Your memory
I'll miss you.

But there will be a time
When I'll see your face,
And I'll hear your voice,
And there we will laugh again.
And there will come a day
When I'll hold you close.
No more tears to cry
'Cause we'll have forever
But I'll say good-bye for now.[4]

Oh the power of singing this song and giving people the word picture of being reunited with their loved ones. What a day that will be for all of us!

One lyric painted such a word picture that lives were saved and hearts tormented by shame and guilt were finally set free. It's called "A Baby's Prayer." I feel as if the divine hand of God truly penned this one.

A Baby's Prayer

I can hear her talking with a friend
I think it's all about me.
Oh how she can't have a baby now.
My mommy doesn't see
That I feel her breathe

I know her voice.
Her blood—it flows through my heart.
God, You know my greatest wish is that
We'd never be apart.

But if I should die before I wake
I pray her soul You'll keep
Forgive her, Lord.
She doesn't know
That You gave life to me.

Not only have I held babies in my arms who were scheduled to be aborted, but I have seen the light come back in women's eyes when they've allowed God to release them from that choice. One extra blessing has come that I didn't even plan on: the song's touching the thousands of women who have had miscarriages. The last verse says this:

On the days when she may think of me
Please comfort her with the truth;
That the angels hold me safe and sound
'Cause I'm in heaven with You.[5]

(Dee) In *The Five Love Languages,* Gary Smalley and John Trent recommend using word pictures to help others understand your feelings. When we were flying home from Thailand with our newly adopted twelve-year-old daughter, Steve remarked on how cute the little boys were in the orphanage. With five children and a ministry, I was feeling overwhelmed. Was he really thinking I could handle more? How could I help my left-brained husband understand? I used a word picture.

"Honey, see that little handle out on the wing? Imagine I am out there, hanging on for dear life, but I am flapping around in the wind and I may lose my grip. I want to keep up with you, but I think I'm going to slip and plummet to my death."

"Is *that* how you are feeling?"

Bingo.

A word picture helped Steve understand my heart. I have learned, from the Lord's model, that if I really want to persuade someone of something, if I really need him to understand, I must come up with an effective word picture.

This is what *The Word* does in Hosea. God's people had been worshiping Him, but they also had other gods in their bed. They simply didn't seem to get it. So "the word of the Lord came to Hosea," giving him an astounding lifetime assignment. He was to marry a woman given to harlotry. Why? Because God needed a picture to penetrate the blind hearts of His people. One commentator writes:

> God could have simply declared: Israel is like a wife to me, an adulterous wife. Instead, He used Hosea to act out the treachery in real life and to show in living color, God's fury, His jealousy, and above all else, His love for His people.[6]

There are those who say, "But God would not command a prophet to marry an immoral woman because He wouldn't link a believer with an unbeliever." We understand the dilemma. It is true that He tells us not to marry unbelievers (see 2 Corinthians 6). However, there are "godly prerogatives." There are some feelings and actions God is allowed that we are not. For example, we are not to be jealous, but God, because He is without sin, can be and is jealous for our devotion.

We are not to take vengeance on one another, but God can and will, because He is holy. Those are "godly prerogatives." These are negatives to us, but with perfect holiness God can use them wisely and justly.

Therefore He could, because He is God, ask a prophet to marry an immoral woman in order to paint a picture, but that certainly does not give us a license to marry unbelievers. James Montgomery Boice writes,

> If Hosea's story cannot be real (because "God could not ask a man to marry an unfaithful woman"), then neither is the story of salvation real, because that is precisely what Christ has done for us. He has purchased us for himself to be a bride "without stain or wrinkle or any other blemish, but holy and blameless" (Eph. 5:27), and he has done this even though he knew in advance that we would often prove faithless.[7]

No doubt, however, God's command came as a surprise to Hosea. Preacher E. F. Bailey imagined the interaction between the Lord and Hosea the day "the word of the Lord" came to the unsuspecting prophet:

> I was making my way back home from one of my many crusades when I descended the heights of Mount Tabor. Suddenly I was apprehended by a strange and invisible presence. . . . I was at once both terrified and fascinated. . . . His voice came to me . . .
>
> "Hosea, I must speak to you concerning the infidelity of My people. You remember our contractual agreement: that Israel would be My people and that I would be her

God. But now, Hosea, because of her apostasy, idolatry, and immorality, her goodness is as the morning dew. . . . She has fractured our friendship, she has ruptured our relationship. . . .

Listening to Him, His voice was the voice of one who had experienced excruciating pain—pain only known to those who have had their love rejected.

"Hosea, I want you to get married. I want you to be My living allegory . . .

"Hosea, I tuned in to several of your last crusades and as I listened to you it was obvious to me that you're not quite ready. . . . You were knowledgeable in theology, eloquent in speech . . . but there was something missing. . . . Hosea, in order to get you ready I am going to send you through the crucible of domestic difficulty."

"Married?" I said. "That's not so bad. Especially when you have an omnicompetent, personal God selecting the bride . . ." I said, "God, it's interesting that You would bring that subject up. Just the other day I was having a conversation with myself and I said, 'Prophet—it's time for you to take on a wife . . .' There is this young lady I've been watching—and I know You know who she is. She comes from an orthodox Jewish background, she's a prophet's child, she comes to all of my crusades. . . . Oh, she'll make a great prophet's wife. . . ."

"Hosea, she's not the one I have in mind. The girl that I have in mind for you is not out of a prophet's family. She's not orthodox. In fact, Hosea, the girl I want you to marry is a pagan prostitute."[8]

There is humor in E. F. Bailey's presentation—unless, perhaps, you have been the victim of infidelity. Then it becomes deadly serious.

This was a *life* sentence, for Hosea prophesied for seventy years, and all during that time, the wife he loved was breaking and rebreaking his heart. One commentator writes:

> Hosea is one of the most emotional books in the Bible, an outpouring of suffering love from God's heart. This shows in the writing, which jumps impulsively from one thought to the next. Read a chapter dramatically aloud, and you will get this sense. It is almost like listening in on a husband-and-wife fight.[9]

Sometimes the Lord will allow one of His children to suffer enormously for the good of the whole body of Christ. Such was the case of Hosea. The Lord had tried to get through to His people with words, but He needed a "living" picture in order to penetrate their hearts. How vital it is that we allow the pictures *The Word* paints to penetrate, to open the eyes of our hearts. Part of meditating on the Word, as Psalm 1 tells us to do, is to put ourselves in the center of these pictures. If you have never experienced infidelity, try to imagine the pain.

The betrayed and abandoned spouse feels the same pain as the one who has lost a spouse to sudden death: the shock, the thoughts of *How will I carry on alone?* Yet some say infidelity is a deeper pain, because the sufferer experiences intentional rejection. Over and over the refrain plays: *I wasn't wanted. I wasn't good enough.*

When you read Hosea's story, you can almost see the tear stains on the pages. The Lord was trying to penetrate His people's dull hearts, to help them wake up and see how their unfaithfulness had caused Him grief.

He pierces our hearts with word pictures because He loves us, and He can see the end result. You see, the Word is not only the Painter, but also the Potter.

YOU ARE THE POTTER

The same God that created our physical lives creates our spiritual lives. And because we are in process, He is continually molding us, fashioning us to be like Him, bringing beauty out of our ashes and joy out of our mourning (see Isaiah 61:3).

One weekend we were at an event where a potter made an urn onstage—a grand and beautiful piece, like you might see at the entrance of a luxurious hotel in Paris. As he worked, he shared his testimony of how God had been continually molding him. We watched him transform a lump of clay before our very eyes. He turned it into a vessel of beauty with delicate etchings. Just as we were all ready to give him a standing ovation, he crushed it down, folding the top within, destroying what we thought was a masterpiece. We gasped. He reached into what was left of the urn and explained that hidden within were ugly scraps of clay that he still had to remove. Just like Jesus, he began a good work and was intent on finishing it. When he finally finished his creation, it was glorious, lovelier than the earlier one he had crushed.

(Kathy) It struck me that each of us was clueless as to what he was creating. Before he even set foot onstage, he knew what the finished work would look like! That was so comforting to me, because many times in His molding my life I've wondered,

> *Where is He taking me?*
> *What is happening?*
> *Am I going to be okay?*

And every time when I look back, I've seen that He was intent on doing a good work in me. He brings beauty from ashes.

It should give us confidence that the same Lord who created this beautiful world out of nothing is at work conforming us to the image of Christ. Does He care? Is He just? Is He wise? Oh yes. Being on the wheel of the Potter may be very painful, but He does indeed know what He is doing.

> When we are unfaithful,
> He is faithful.
>
> When we forget Him,
> He remembers us.
>
> When we run away,
> He pursues us.

He has begun a good work in us, and the Word will bring it to completion, even if it means taking us through the fire.

I've sung songs with words like "You are the Potter; I am the clay," for years, but to actually see this man onstage as if he were in his workshop was life changing. He was Jesus, and I was the clay. Whenever I used to picture a potter, I thought of two hands delicately sculpting a piece of art. Fingers and hands moved with artistic, graceful precision. But as he molded the clay, it was much more involved than that. There was an intense and bold determination as he was hugging and holding the clay. His face never softened in its concentration. He aggressively threw his whole body into the work, and yet, it was such a tender sight. There was a love in him for the piece he was creating. I almost felt as if my watching was intrusive. Not only were his hands and arms covered with clay, but also, one side of his face got completely smeared. His cheek was helping to balance the object of his heart.

(*Dee*) It almost reminded me of the act of making love: sometimes tender, sometimes intense, but totally encompassing, embracing, and loving. *Seeing* this helped me to realize that though being on the Potter's wheel can be painful, it is *always* good, for He truly loves us.

When we adopted our daughter Anne, our older daughter Sally went into a full-blown depression. At the time, I wondered: *What have we done? Have we made a mistake?* We had a beautiful family. But it seemed it was crumbling before my eyes. I didn't have a vision for the future, but God did. And just like the potter we were watching, God was so close. Out of the intense heat and stretching, God removed things we hadn't even been able to see and built an even stronger and more loving family. Now, as we walk through Steve's cancer, there are many times when grief wells up in me, and I cannot imagine how I will survive. The heat seems too intense, the pain too sharp, the future too bleak. But when I remember that look of concentration and love in the potter's eyes, I can yield.

There is an important, and, for some, a controversial theme threaded throughout Scripture: we have freedom to make choices in some areas, but some areas God completely determines. We are a people who like always to be in control. When we hear that God may harden a heart, or choose a people for Himself, or put a righteous man over the fire, we may bristle and say: "That's not fair!" But Paul, in quoting Hosea in Romans 9, a passage we will look at in the workbook, sternly rebuked that kind of arrogant thinking and asked,

> Is God unrighteous?
> Does not the Potter have power over the clay?

How can we argue with the wisdom of a holy God? We must humble ourselves before Him and realize that the God who made the universe is smarter than we are. He is not obligated to us. We are at His mercy, but He is righteous.

Change My Heart, O God

The Potter who changes the clay from a lump into a beautiful work of art is the Word who created man from the dust of the earth and is fashioning him and conforming him into the image of Christ. Essential to the process is water. As we watched the potter in action on stage, he often wet his hands with water and moistened the clay. How exciting it was to realize that the Word uses His word to keep us pliable. How often do we say, "I'm so dry"? If we don't allow the Word to water us, He won't be able to accomplish His purposes for us.

It has become a habit of my life to pray through Psalms, a habit that has sustained me in this time of suffering. Without this habit, I think the heat of our circumstances could cause me to become brittle, but the water of the Word has kept me pliable in His hands. A few years ago, when Steve and I were going through another valley, because our daughter was in a very difficult marriage, I was writing *A Woman's Journey through Psalms,* a Bible study I was doing with Integrity Music. They were providing the CD with the Psalms set to music, and I was writing the guide. Steve said to me one morning, "Would you ask Integrity if they have a song on Psalm 119:49–50? It has been ministering to me so deeply as we pray for our daughter."

Though I did not think it likely, I e-mailed them. They wrote back excitedly that they did, and it was one of their favorite praise songs. The words of the psalm, and the song, are these:

Remember the [W]ord to Your servant,
Upon which You have caused me to hope.
This is my comfort in my affliction,
For Your [W]ord has given me life.[10]

God loves it when we remind Him about His promises. Of course, it is not that the Lord has forgotten, but He loves to know that *we* have not forgotten. Often, when I remind the Lord of one of His promises, it gives Him the opportunity to dialogue with me. As I pray through the promise, I see something in it I had not seen before—often something that calls for a response from me before I can expect a response from the Lord. If I allow the Word to splash water on me, then the Potter can work with me and turn the dry ashes of my heart and life into something beautiful. In our personal situation, in the matter of our daughter's marriage, God had mercy. He not only rescued our daughter, but He also refined her and refined us as her parents.

The same Word that hovered over the face of the deep in Genesis longs to hover over us and to make us women of beauty.

The next portrait we will study is that of *The Bridegroom.* Some have misunderstood our excitement over Jesus being our Bridegroom, and we are eager to address this misunderstanding right away—but then show you why this portrait has been so meaningful to believers throughout the ages.

THE BROKENHEARTED
BRIDEGROOM

The Brokenhearted Bridegroom
Artist: Martin French (www.martinfrench.com)

It is a bold and creative stroke by which God, instead of banning sexual imagery from religion, rescues and raises it to portray the ardent love and fidelity which are the essence of His covenant. Having made that clear, He can now go on to show what concord and delight the full flowering of that marriage God and man will bring.

—DEREK KIDNER

5

The Brokenhearted Bridegroom

*S*o many of you have written to tell us how the Falling in Love with Jesus series has transformed your lives. Yet a few have wondered about approaching Jesus as their Bridegroom and have asked thoughtful questions. Even though God Himself uses sexual imagery in the Song of Solomon and Hosea to help us understand His longing for faithfulness and devotion, we understand how strange it may seem. You wonder, *Is this appropriate?* We also understand that some of you have been told that the term "the bride" applies only to the corporate body of the church, and not to us as individuals. You wonder, *Is this true?*

It seems clear that we need to address these and other legitimate questions before we can proceed with the portrait given in Hosea and John of Jesus as our Bridegroom.

Is the portrait of Jesus as our Bridegroom scriptural?

Other than the portrait of God as our Father, the portrait of Jesus as our Bridegroom is one writers of the Old and New Testaments painted more frequently than any other. The Bible opens with a "marriage" (Adam and Eve) and closes with a "wedding ceremony" (Christ, "the second Adam" coming on a white horse for His bride). In between are whole books devoted to the concept, such as the Song of Solomon and Hosea. Isaiah and Jeremiah are filled with pictures of our Bridegroom and of us, often as an unfaithful bride. Hidden in Psalm 45, the book of Ruth, and many other passages is Jesus, our Kinsman-Redeemer Husband, our royal Bridegroom. Jesus told not one, but *many* parables about a bridegroom, a great wedding feast, and virgins who were not ready. Paul told us that earthly marriages are a picture of a much deeper reality, the mystery of the relationship of Christ with His bride, the church.

What is the main message we should gain from Jesus as our Bridegroom?

The Lord longs to help us understand that His heart is not for the rules and regulations of religion, but for a relationship of ardent devotion. God is looking for true worshipers who will keep a covenant relationship with Him. He rejoices over us, and it breaks His heart to be forgotten, to see us running after other lovers, reducing our relationship to ritual, breaking our "marriage vows."

But isn't there a sexual connotation that is inappropriate?

Anytime a portrait is given to help us understand a holy God, it is possible to press certain aspects too far, distorting the meaning.

Because we've talked about intimacy with God in this series, it has sometimes broken our hearts that some have been able to equate deep intimacy *only* with sex. God *does* use sexual images to convey a point, for, after all, He created sex, but it is always in the purest and holiest sense. He desires oneness with us. He has made a covenant with us. He has betrothed us to Himself. In Hosea, He says,

> *I will betroth you to Me in faithfulness,*
> *And you shall know the LORD.*
>
> —HOSEA 2:20

Paul told us to keep ourselves pure until our *Bridegroom* returns, explaining,

> *For I am jealous for you with godly jealousy. For I have betrothed you to one husband, that I may present you as a chaste virgin to Christ.*
>
> —2 CORINTHIANS 11:2

Throughout the ages, God's bride has struggled with purity. She looks for love in all the wrong places. In Hosea, we read,

> *"She decked herself with her earrings and jewelry,*
> *And went after her lovers,*
> *But Me she forgot," says the LORD.*
>
> —HOSEA 2:13

Derek Kidner's explanation is vital, worthy of repeating:

> It is a bold and creative stroke by which God, instead of banning sexual imagery from religion, rescues and raises

it to portray the ardent love and fidelity which are the essence of His covenant.[1]

Still, for many, the use of sexual images in Scripture is upsetting. We believe this is because our world has polluted the beauty of the marriage bed. Sexual immorality is rampant and images of impurity flow, like a sewer, into our minds and hearts. And yet the holiness of the sexual union between a husband and wife has not changed. God still says: "Marriage is honorable among all, and the bed undefiled" (Hebrews 13:4). Clearly, again, marriage is a dim reflection of a deeper reality, that of Christ and His bride.

(*Kathy*) Even as a single woman, I understand the portrait. I may not have a husband, but I am living in the "deeper reality." I am the bride of Christ. I do not have an earthly sexual partner, but just as married women can understand the spiritual analogy, so can I. That is such a joy to me, knowing I am in covenant with the living God. Jesus meets the deepest needs of my soul and tenderly directs me through this life.

When I met the Lord, I was very much aware of Him as my *Bridegroom,* even more so than as my Father. I told Dee that, as a young believer, I wrote a song called "Mr. Tenderness." It was when I first took a glimpse of the pictures in Song of Solomon. In my new-found love for Christ, and His love for me, I was overwhelmed by the fact that He desired deep intimacy with me. His calling me "Beloved" awakened my soul in a way I had not known, and, based on pictures from this Song, I wrote my own song, one that shows intimacy is about relationship.

MR. TENDERNESS

Your left hand under your little girl's head,
Your right hand embracing me Sweet Beloved.

We are skipping over mountains,
bounding over hills.
I'm sitting in the shadows to be led where You will.
Your tenderness . . . Mr. Tenderness . . .

Awake O South Wind,
Awake O North Wind,
Spread the fragrance of my love for Him.
He leads me to His garden
with a glance of His eyes
to eat of all the good fruit while walking by His side.

Arise, my Love;
My fair one come away
Is what You said to me
on our lovely wedding day?
Now I'll cling to all Your promises
Your love has set me free
I am my Beloved's
His desire is for me.
Your tenderness . . . Mr. Tenderness

In the morning I arise
to see the loving in Your eyes
so tender to me.
And at the setting of the sun
I'm still embraced by my Loved One
So tenderly . . .[2]

We understand that not everyone is going to be comfortable with the portrait of Jesus as *Bridegroom*, just as not everyone is comfortable with the portrait of God as Father. We tend to process spiritual things by our human experiences. If we have had negative earthly role models or painful experiences, seeing the Lord as Husband or as Father will be difficult for us. But God is so good. In the process of our growing in relationship with Him, healing starts to happen, and we relate to God in ways He has so desired. In fact, one day, the portrait we pushed away may become the most meaningful one of all. In the meantime, let us give one another grace, as we all are at different points in our journey to the high places.

Is the portrait of Jesus as our Bridegroom only for Israel?

In Hosea, God was specifically addressing Israel. But in Hosea we also see the wonderful promise, the mystery, fulfilled in the New Testament, that God was going to make a people who were not His people, His people. Not only would believing Israel be His bride, but the way would be open to Gentiles who believe as well. The pleadings in Hosea are not just for Israel, but for each of us who believes.

Does the portrait of Jesus as our Bridegroom apply only to the corporate bride, and not to us as individuals?

There are three pictures in Ephesians to describe the body of believers: a building, a body, and a bride. In each, there is an individual and a corporate application. Consider, for example, the building, or temple. Each one of us is, indeed, the temple of the Holy Spirit (1 Corinthians 6:19). Yet this picture also represents all of God's people (Ephesians 2:19–22). With the picture of the body, the hand should not say, "Jesus is talking to the whole body, so this isn't relevant to me, the hand." Yet the hand should also understand the value

of the eye, and of cooperating with the eye, and of ı.
superior to the eye.

In the same way, the portrait of the bride is clearly ı.
ual (as in the Song of Solomon) and corporate (as iı
However, even when a Scripture writer is addressing the chu.
porately, there is always an individual application. It would be a
evasion to say, "God isn't asking me, personally, to be faithful—ı.
message is for the church." When John wrote, "God so loved the
world," it doesn't mean that God doesn't love us as individuals. God
is so personal that He knows our names, the number of hairs on our
heads, and our innermost thoughts. When He tells us He loves us,
when He tells us He wants us to be faithful, He is talking to us as
individuals, who make up the entire body of believers.

Yet in emphasizing the individual aspect of this picture, it is easy
to fall into the other error: neglecting the corporate picture. One
young woman wisely observed: "So often women have a tendency
not to get along with other women—to feel intimidated, to be easily
hurt, to be jealous—so they withdraw from their responsibility to the
body of Christ. Since Christ is preparing a bride that is to be without
spot or wrinkle, the goal is for the *whole* bride to be that way."
Another woman observed, "Sometimes individuals will not see the
need to be involved in godly community and the local church. They
fail to see that this is a primary way the Lord has provided for them.
They'll justify their lack of involvement by emphasizing that they
don't need church to love God: 'I'm okay. Jesus is with me.'"

While the picture of *The Bridegroom* may be particularly meaningful to us as individuals, and particularly to us as women, it is vital
to remember the corporate aspect. The bride of Christ is made up of
all believers: Jews, Gentiles, singles, marrieds, men, women, and
children. There is a beauty in corporate worship, for example, that

e cannot achieve alone. There is a beauty in loving one another that we cannot achieve alone. There is a beauty in sharpening one another, in holding one another accountable, in praying for and supporting one another, in coming under the protection of a local church, that we cannot achieve alone. If we are not actively involved in the body of Christ, we are *not* a beautiful bride.

When John saw "the Holy City, the New Jerusalem, coming down out of heaven from God, prepared as a bride beautifully dressed for her husband" (Revelation 21:2 NIV), he was seeing the *entire* bride of Christ, in all her many-faceted colors, made up of every tribe and nation, loving one another in holy harmony.

We understand the injustices and hurts that many have experienced with Christians. You can really get to the point where you don't want anything to do with them. But no matter how hypocritical, sick, or healthy the body of Christ has been through the ages, it is *still* and always will be His body, and the gates of hell will not prevail against it. Scripture is clear that we need each other and that forsaking being together grieves and angers the Lord.

Just how literal is Scripture being when it talks about Jesus as our Bridegroom?

Obviously there were times when Jesus spoke in metaphors. When He wept over Jerusalem, saying He wished He could gather her as a mother hen gathers her chicks under her wings, we know He was speaking metaphorically. We also have learned that the Word likes to paint pictures to penetrate the heart. So, just how literally can we take the pictures of a wedding feast, a Bridegroom coming on a white horse for His bride, or the Lord rejoicing over us with singing?

The picture of *The Bridegroom* is a primary one, as is the portrait of the Father. How literal is it? It is much more than a metaphor, but it is also a mystery. Read carefully what Paul wrote about this picture:

> *"For this reason a man will leave his father and mother and be united to his wife, and the two will become one flesh." This is a profound mystery—but I am talking about Christ and the church.*
>
> —EPHESIANS 5:31–32 NIV

It *is* a profound mystery, but certainly an enthralling one, and not to be dismissed. When we are uncertain as to just how literally we are to apply a poetic picture, it is always vital to come back to the main point of the picture. In this case, as we have said, we can absolutely know that God has a profound love affair with His people and longs for a responsive, faithful bride.

Now, let us begin to look closely at this in Hosea and John.

JESUS, LOVER OF MY SOUL

If you have experienced betrayal by a spouse, best friend, or close family member, then you know there is no pain like it. When you are knit together with someone, whether in body or in soul, and a severing occurs, it tears at your very being. You are unable to sleep, to concentrate, to keep the tears from flowing. You keep thinking, *How could they do this after I have loved them so well and so long? I would have laid down my life for them—and now, this?*

(Dee) When I was a little girl, a very pleasant woman came to our house every Friday to do our ironing. Mrs. Hahn sang as she ironed or listened with a smile to my childish chatter. I remember visiting her at her simple home. Money was tight for her family, and her husband's job required him to be away a great deal, but she had made it a little piece of heaven, complete with ruffled curtains, candles, and the fragrance of homemade bread. She spoke lovingly of her husband, and it seemed an ideal marriage.

But when he died we discovered that, for forty years, he had lived a double life: he had a wife and children in another state. The money Mrs. Hahn had taken home from ironing, he had spent on another family. The nights she had given up with him, he had given to another. The covenant she had honored, he had trampled upon. When she discovered his lifelong treachery, it was as if her kite, which once soared, took a sudden dive.

She still came to our home, but she no longer sang or smiled or listened attentively to my chatter. When I think about how she must have felt, I can better understand the emotion and contradicting statements in Hosea. I can picture Mrs. Hahn thinking, after she discovered her husband's infidelity, *I was not his wife, and he was not my husband!* And yet, she *was* his wife, and he *was* her husband. Mrs. Hahn helps me understand the statements in Hosea, when God accused His bride in court and cried:

> Rebuke your mother, rebuke her,
> for she is not my wife,
> and I am not her husband.
>
> —HOSEA 2:2 NIV

Of course we are His wife, and He is our Husband, but oh, how the love can go out of our relationship because of our infidelities. It is also important to see that it is here, when the Lord said, "I am not her husband," that He was saying, "For a time, I will not be the Great I AM to My people," for the words are the same as the "I AMs" in Exodus and in John.

It may seem odd, as Max Lucado writes, "to think of God as an enthralled lover . . . as a suitor intoxicated on love."[3] Yet that is how He paints Himself, a picture intended to penetrate our hearts, and in Hosea, the Brokenhearted Bridegroom's heart is broken—sometimes He weeps, sometimes He rages. Nothing seems to trouble the Lord more than being forgotten and betrayed by the one for whom He has sacrificed so much. If you don't really care for someone, you are not terribly hurt if he does not care for you. But as Charles Spurgeon observed:

> This, then, is clear proof that God greatly loves his people, since, whenever their hearts wander from him, he is greatly grieved.[4]

The scene in Hosea 2 is a divorce court! As we've said before, this will not truly be divorce, but separation. But still, *for now,* the marriage is over.

> *Put your mother on trial, plead with her!*
> *(For she is no wife of mine and I am not her husband.)*
> *Tell her to wash the paint from her face,*
> *And the seductions from between her breasts*
> —HOSEA 2:2 PHILLIPS

R. C. Sproul says, "You can almost hear Hosea thinking, *God, how can You say, 'I'm going to divorce My people'? . . . You betrothed Yourself to these people forever. . . . It was a 'death do us part.' . . . How can You even think about divorce, even with the apostasy of the nation?*" So what is God saying? Sproul says God cries, "I'm saying both! You are not my people, and yet, still, [and you sense the anguish, how He cannot let her go] you *are* my people."[5] Derek Kidner sees it like this: "God is not saying that

He is going back on His marriage covenant, for the whole thrust of Hosea is that God will not go back on His marriage vows. What He is saying instead is, 'The reality has gone out of our relationship.'"[6]

In the story of Hosea, this "separation" was a literal prophecy concerning God's people. Shortly after Hosea's prophecy, invading armies captured God's people and scattered and oppressed them. How far God must have seemed from them! Did Hosea's words come back to them? Surely, they must have, as well as the words that gave them hope. Repentance would lead to reconciliation and a renewal of the marriage vows.

Separation, as painful as it is, can be tough love for the wronged spouse. We see this in earthly marriages. It is hard to separate from someone you love, even if that person is being unfaithful or has an addiction that is destroying both of you. But often the only hope for healing is in separation, and in insisting that the wayward spouse get help and bear the fruit of repentance before you take him back.

True love is sacrificial. On a spiritual level, God didn't want to give up Israel, even for a time, but He had to, to bring her to her senses. He was willing to bring the law down on her, even to the point of exposing her hidden sins, so that she would give up her destructive behavior. In Scripture, we see God withdrawing and being silent when His people have been unfaithful to Him.

In Christ Alone

What was it exactly that made the Lord so angry with His bride in the book of Hosea? We've touched on this in previous chapters, but let's take another look. In court, He used her own words to accuse her:

> *For she said, "I will go after my lovers,*
> *Who give me my bread and my water,*

My wool and my linen,
My oil and my drink."

—Hosea 2:5

Israel's particular sin was the age-old sin of syncretism (mixing and merging of one religion with another). Syncretism is derived from the words "sin" and "creed." While she (Israel) claimed to worship the Lord, there were other gods "in her bed," for she also worshiped Baal and the gods of the culture around her.

There is more to Hosea 2:5 than might at first be apparent. The gods of Canaan, such as Baal, were largely patrons of fertility. To get the best results from these gods or "husbands," as they were sometimes called, the people performed sexual acts in the temple, thinking this inspired these gods to give them fertile herds and crops. The people felt that the God of Abraham, Isaac, and Jacob was somehow out of His element, so they had to turn to less noble gods, and those gods became addictive. Derek Kidner explains,

> There was the fascination of the forbidden and decadent—the exciting exchange of Yahweh's broad daylight for the twilight world of violent gods, with their raw passions, cruelties, and ecstasies; an exchange which has a perennial appeal.[7]

We've seen, as Derek Kidner says, "a modern dethroning of God" in today's church. In certain issues of today's culture, Yahweh seems to be somewhat out of His realm. It's almost as if we say, "Yes, I understand that God is omnipotent, omnipresent, and omniscient, but . . ." Throughout the history of the church, His people have often felt that God wasn't quite enough. As Kidner says,

These beliefs are not as foreign or remote from our age as they might seem. The idea that God has little relevance to the natural world is taken for granted by the secularized majority.[8]

In Hosea's day, Israel turned to violent gods. Christians who want to lose weight or stop smoking have turned to hypnotists. People may say they trust Jesus, but then, because He isn't telling them all they want to know about the future, they turn to astrology or mysticism. There is the feeling: *I need a little more help here.*

(Dee) One year a well-known New Age speaker was scheduled to speak at a women's retreat at a mainline denomination in Lincoln, Nebraska. The day before the event she became very ill. The coordinator called me in a panic and said, "This woman was going to take us higher—do you think you could do that for us?"

I said, "I certainly know the God who can."

When I spoke, I shared how Jesus had changed my life and I presented the gospel clearly. As soon as I named Jesus, some looked down, studying the carpet, but others had faces full of longing, eager to embrace the truth. Afterward, I read their church bulletin, describing their choice of Sunday school classes. They offered some good Bible studies with materials from Max Lucado and Chuck Swindoll. But they also offered New Age classes, mysticism, and yoga. Just as in Hosea's day, these people who claimed the name of the one true God had other "gods" in their bed. This is religious syncretism.

Many individuals belong to Bible-believing churches yet are also members of secret societies such as Freemasonry, a religion whose tenets are in opposition to Christianity. Freemasons believe there are many ways to God, including Buddha or Allah.[9] Jesus is called a teacher, a man, or a legend—but never God.[10] They believe one can get to heaven through good works that will lead them to the "Grand Lodge on High." The Freemasonry Bible says hell is temporary.[11] How can one embrace both Christianity and Freemasonry? You cannot. Though members would say there is no conflict, the Lord would disagree.

We will return to Hosea in a moment, but it is interesting to see that the gospel of John also provides a picture of how God longs for a pure bride, a chaste virgin who is faithful to Christ alone. You may be surprised at the Jewish wedding customs, but we believe you will also find them profoundly intriguing.

FRIEND OF THE BRIDEGROOM

In John's gospel, John the Baptist made it very clear that he was not the Bridegroom, but "the friend of the bridegroom" (John 3:29). What did he mean? Here's a little excerpt from our conversation one day:

"Kath, did you know that in those days, the consummation of the sexual relationship didn't happen on the honeymoon?"

"Dee, unfortunately, that's not news in the twenty-first century."

"No, Kath, I mean it happened during the wedding reception."

"*What* happened during the wedding reception?"

"The consummation."

"Are you saying what I think you are saying?"

"I'm saying to you that during the wedding reception, the couple consummated their sexual relationship in a wedding hut. The guests waited outside."

"The guests waited outside. Hmm. I mean, after all this time I've been single, can you imagine my friends and my family waiting right outside my hotel room door? I don't think so."

Yet that is exactly what happened. The "friend of the bridegroom" had several responsibilities. The first was to assure that the wedding hut or bridal chamber was in order. Then, after the bride and groom were carried up in the air with joy and singing to this hut, the "friend of the bridegroom" waited outside for the bridegroom to call him to take the blood-stained cloth that was proof of the bride's virginity.[12] Finally, if, after the marriage there were problems between the husband and wife, he was to act as a counselor.[13]

John Calvin saw all ministers of the gospel as "friends of the Bridegroom" who help assure the purity and fidelity of the bride and the health of her marriage to the Bridegroom.[14]

Though these customs may seem strange, when we look at them on a symbolic level, representing God's great desire for a pure and chaste bride who is devoted to Him alone, they become understandable.

HOLY, HOLY, HOLY

Some husbands, when their wives are unfaithful, will simply put up with it, for they fear losing them completely. (The same is true with women when their husbands are unfaithful.) A true lover seeks the other's best, even if it means risking that individual's affection.

Our Lord is not like that. He will not put up with infidelity. And we have an extremely creative Bridegroom. After all, He is the Word who created the galaxies. Since in Hosea He had married an unfaithful bride (Israel), He was going to re-create her as a pure and faithful woman. If one method failed, He would use another. In Hosea 2 we see Him taking His time in order to win a response that will make the reconciliation genuine.

BREAK MY HEART

After accusing her "in court," He began to help her get back on the narrow road, the highway to holiness. His first method was to line the exit ramps:

> *Therefore, behold,*
> *I will hedge up your way with thorns.*
>
> —Hosea 2:6

God will allow us to feel the sharp consequences of our rebellious ways to awaken us, much like what happened in the story of the prodigal son, when he ended up in poverty, eating pigs' food. It was so painful that he wanted to get back on the narrow road that led to his father. Think of the consequences of sexual immorality, gluttony, laziness, or whatever sin beckons you. These consequences are thorns, gifts from a loving Bridegroom.

(*Dee*) One evening my daughter Sally and I had a discussion about this. The next morning she went outside, saying she wanted to have a little time with God. When she came in, I asked, "Did you receive a 'kiss from the King'?"

"In a way I did. He opened my eyes to something. I've been bowing to a god called 'Dozing Comfort.'"

"What do you mean?"

"Oh Mom, I've been losing so much of the morning because I can't get out of bed. I realized today that the morning is so sweet—I love my time with Him then, and I get so much more done. The consequences of losing all that, I realized, are thorns from God. When He showed me this, it made me willing to destroy that 'god' in my life."

If thorns will not block our determined pursuit of false lovers, our *Bridegroom* has a second strategy. In addition to the hedge of thorns, He may build a wall, a sweet protection shielding us from temptation and trial.

(*Kathy*) Many times I've gotten a morning phone call from a dear friend: "Kath, I was up in the middle of the night, just really disturbed in my spirit. I prayed for you for quite some time. Are you okay? I feel as if something or someone is trying to bring you down. It feels dangerous. Maybe you can pray about it, because if it is God telling me this, it might save you from a lot of trouble and turmoil."

It will be interesting, when we see Jesus face to face, to learn all the times He was a Sun and a Shield to us, when He sent angels to protect us, when He put an invisible hedge about us to shield us from danger or temptation.

Yet there are times when we crash through the thorns, charge through the hedge, and are determined to do things our way. In Hosea, the Lord had to strip His bride of her blessings, taking away her grain, new wine, wool, and linen. Her vineyards became forests for the wild beasts. Yet all of these disciplines He intended to "be corrective wrath designed to bring His people back, to lead them to repentance that the covenant may be renewed."[15]

Amazing Love

In the next chapter you will see a wonderful turn in Hosea, where the strategy of the Lord becomes the allurement of love. Many of the pictures and phrases remind us of an earthly bridegroom who woos his bride, who speaks tenderly to her, who delights her so much that she opens to him. God intended marriage, both on an earthly level between husband and wife, and also on a spiritual level between Christ and His bride, to be a love song, a dance. We will be considering one of our favorite passages in all of Hosea and the key passage for *Forever in Love with Jesus*:

Therefore, behold, I will allure her,
Will bring her into the wilderness,
And speak comfort to her.
I will give her her vineyards from there,
And the Valley of Achor as a door of hope;
She shall sing there,
As in the days of her youth,
As in the day when she came up from the land of Egypt.
—HOSEA 2:14–15

The allurement of love. The dance. Like two eagles in the sky. Like the way of a man with a maiden (Proverbs 30:18–19).

THE BETROTHING
BRIDEGROOM

The Betrothing Bridegroom
Artist: Martin French (www.martinfrench.com)

Other forms of power had been tried upon Israel . . . He said to her,

"I will hedge up thy way with thorns;" but she went right over the

thorns. Then he said, "I will make a wall, that she shall not find her

paths;" but she broke through the wall . . . Though she found no

mirth in sin, and the way of her transgressions was hard, yet Israel

would not turn to God; but the sweet allurement of tenderness would

succeed where all else had failed.

—CHARLES SPURGEON

6

The Betrothing Bridegroom

Kathy) My closest friends were so gracious to throw me a housewarming party when I moved to Nashville. I was humbled at the idea of it; single women don't have the sweet experience of friends throwing showers for them. To think I could go to some of my favorite stores, make a list of all the things I loved in those stores, and have my friends go and buy them for me. Was it really going to happen?

Off I went to register at some of those stores, looking at kitchen, bed, and bath things galore. I was standing in Williams-Sonoma, checking out the array of kitchen utensils I knew I would never use—I boil a mean pot of water—but that I knew other people would need if they cooked at my house. While looking at the knives, I suddenly felt overwhelmed. *What do I know about carving, paring, and filleting? I just need something that cuts well.* So I asked a store clerk for some help. I told her I was registering, so she took out a form to help me mark some items. The first thing she said was,

"Well, most brides . . ."

A pain hit my heart I don't usually feel. As most of you know, I've often described my contentment in my singleness. For some reason, that day her words pierced me far more than the knives I was looking at could have.

> *Wow. I have never, and might not ever, experience being a bride.*

My friend Glenna was with me, and she tapped me on the shoulder as my eyes welled up with tears. She's a little bit older than me and has been part of my prayer team, so she knows some of my deepest heart. She whispered,

> "You *are* a bride."

How ironic that I've written and spoken to thousands of women about this, boldly proclaiming my betrothment. Because I was taken off guard, it was such a tender moment to be gently reminded that I was His. An unspoken joy came back in my heart that helped me finish my registering, knowing that my Bridegroom was with me.

HIS BANNER OVER ME IS LOVE

He loves me with an everlasting love. Isaiah said:

> *And as the bridegroom rejoices over the bride,*
> *So shall your God rejoice over you.*
>
> —ISAIAH 62:5

Zephaniah said,

> The Mighty One, will save;
> He will rejoice over you with gladness,
> He will quiet you with His love,
> He will rejoice over you with singing.
>
> —ZEPHANIAH 3:17

Hosea said,

> I will . . . speak tenderly to her.
>
> —HOSEA 2:14 NIV

When Paul was speaking of how husbands should cherish their wives and how wives should respond to those husbands with respect, suddenly he made a shift from the earthly love relationship to the spiritual one and said,

> This is a great mystery, but I speak concerning Christ and the church.
>
> —EPHESIANS 5:32

The mystery is that, just as in an earthly marriage the secret has to do with the heart instead of "rules," so it is with Christ and the church.

(Dee) My brother-in-law, John Frahm, has been a pastor, has taught at a Christian college, and heads up Alpha (a ministry God is using mightily in evangelism and revival) on North American campuses. But though he was sound doctrinally, it wasn't until he became involved in Alpha that his understanding about Jesus truly went from his head to his heart. He told me recently:

"Falling in love with Jesus—that's really what it is all about. I was watching an Alpha video for about the third time when I suddenly found myself weeping. It was tremendous joy, and yet sorrow, at discovering this so late in life: that the Lord loves me so tenderly, and that this life is all about relationship with Him.

"I thought about my relationship with my wife, Sally, and how hurt I would be if she just came to me with a list of things she wanted me to do for her instead of expressing her affection and the desire to be with me. Everything is changing for me: my prayer time—I spend much more time in adoration, in song; my attitude—I'm understanding the concept of 'practicing His presence.'"

THE LOVE OF MY LIFE

God uses pictures to turn the light on for us, and because we seem to grasp the beauty of earthly love, He uses that picture to help us understand what He longs for from us. Who wants a marriage that is about duty, drudgery, and dollars? When we look at our marriages like that, they become a tremendous burden, and we feel trapped.

In *The Mystery of Marriage*, Mike Mason tells of how doubts plagued him on his honeymoon. After visiting a Trappist monastery with his new bride, he began to wonder if marriage was a terrible mistake for him. The finality of it all seized him. What had he done? Was he hopelessly trapped? Was it really too late to back out? He and his bride drove away through fields of ripe blond wheat, the silence between them "eerie and agonizing." Then, high above in the blue sky, two dots were circling around each other:

"Hawks," said my wife.
"Yes, hawks," I said.

The pair were still very high up, but as they drew closer to us they began to descend in great lazy swoops down the blue invisible banisters of the air. It looked as if they were coming down especially for the purpose of putting on a show for us. I parked the car, and we got out to watch. . . .

The longer we watched, the clearer it became that these hawks were doing absolutely nothing of practical import . . . they were simply playing. They were enjoying the warm blueness of the day, the strength and the skill in their wings, the fun of flying, (and perhaps most of all) the fun of each other. . . . There was something in this soaring dance of the pair of them, with a whole sky all to themselves, which spoke directly to me, not just of play and freedom on a summer's day, but of all the shining beauty of love, the pure ease and joy of companionship.[1]

The Lord used that picture to remind Mike of the glory of love, and of His power for the married life. It could be, indeed, wonderful and glorifying to God.

But what does Mike's story have to do with Jesus and us?

In a mysterious way, a beautiful earthly marriage and the hawks' dance of love are pictures of the relationship Jesus has with His bride. Too often people equate Christianity with ethical behavior, with good works, with being good people; and while these *follow* the essence of Christianity, they are not *the* essence. It begins and should continue to be, primarily, a love affair, a playful companionship, like two hawks in the sky. As in every earthly marriage, there will be hard times, but our Husband is perfect, and He longs for a responsive bride.

There is a turn now in Hosea. The Lord, the Bridegroom of Israel, had charged her "in court." He had allowed the thorns of her sin to pierce her. He had taken away her vineyards. He had exposed her in the eyes of her lovers. He had moved away from her for a time. Still, her heart was hard. She was not responding to Him.

Though she deserved to be abandoned, He did not forsake her. Softly and tenderly, He began to woo her. Where? Into the wilderness! There she would be alone with Him, away from her other lovers.

We can see an illustration of this in Israel's delivery from slavery in Egypt. At first she was a grateful bride, for when the Red Sea closed over her enemies, Miriam took up her timbrel and led all the women in song. But soon Israel forgot the Lord's great mercies. She murmured, she complained. He could see her hardening heart, but even though she had betrayed Him, He did not give up. He led her on a long journey into the wilderness, where she was completely dependent on Him to sustain her. He fed her, He guided her, and He loved her. His purpose was to win her heart again.

We've mentioned that in Hosea's day, Israel's sin was religious syncretism. It was a form of idolatry, worshiping other gods in addition to the only true God. We do this today both corporately and individually.

Perhaps you are thinking, *I don't worship other gods.* Perhaps your doctrine is sound, and you are immersed enough in the Word and good expositional preaching that the philosophies of other religions are not leading you astray. However, we need to look clearly at our lives to see where our trust is. Often, it is in ourselves, making us unduly concerned with our reputations. It may be in our wealth or in various comforts we place in our lives. God may have to take them away to show us what unreliable gods these are. But most often, as women, we are prone to trust in people, to cling to them too tightly, and to idolize them, much as the Israelites idolized Baal.

Above All

Some of you may know the story of Sheldon Vanauken ("Van") and his young wife, Davy. Their story was so romantic. They lived on a sailboat they named *Grey Goose*. Because the grey goose was monogamous, when his mate died, he flew on alone for the rest of his life. This couple decided not to have children because they didn't want to share each other with anyone. Sounds severe, doesn't it?

Davy died much sooner than either could have ever imagined. We both found it interesting that they called the love bond between them "the shining barrier." That is a beautiful phrase for two people in love, because you truly don't want anything to get between the two of you, but two *believers* in love should continually focus on *Jesus's* being "the shining barrier" between them. That's when a couple can exchange the highest and purest love.

After Davy died, Van slowly began to cast off much of the slumber that had held him in this fairy tale. His primary focus had been on his wife. C. S. Lewis wrote to him, calling it "a severe mercy" that Davy was taken from him, for Van truly did worship her and put her above God. They had lived in a severe state of idolatry.

The Solid Rock

(Dee) As Steve battles extensive cancer, I have often thought of Vanauken's book *A Severe Mercy*. So few seem to be blessed with a precious and unfailing earthly love, and I am overwhelmed with thankfulness that Steve and I have received this. I do not take for granted the years I have had with this godly man. Even now, with this formidable diagnosis, nothing in his attitude has changed. He is still praying, still singing hymns, still loving everyone in his path, still attentively listening and responding to people's needs, still gentle, still laughing. Jesus is so alive in him.

As a young woman, I did expect Steve to be what only God could be to me, and the Lord had to awaken me to my idolatry. As women, because we are gifted to be relational, we have such a tendency toward dependency: with our husbands, our friends, even our children. I remember how I wrestled with this in my own life in my thirties. I was jealous when my best friend got another good friend. My budding growth in this area produced *The Friendships of Women*. This is what I wrote almost twenty years ago in that book. These words have come flooding back to me since Steve's diagnosis:

> As I've been considering this whole issue of feminine dependency, I have been observing our daughter and her friend Tricia. They are practically joined at the hip. As I am writing this it is summer, and the two have seldom been apart. They zip their sleeping bags together, share their Popsicles, and even, when pressed, borrow each other's underwear and toothbrushes. When they are sepa-rated, I sense Sally's anxiety. They have told me they will absolutely die if they don't get in the same class next year.
>
> Pondering their friendship, I ask, "Do you think you are dependent on each other?"
>
> "What does 'dependent' mean?" Tricia asks.

Searching quickly for a simple synonym, I say, "Do you think you need each other?"

In unison they chime, "YES!"

Seeing my perturbed pause, Sally questions, "Is that bad?"

"Well," I respond, "we should be dependent on Jesus."

"Can't I be dependent on Jesus and Tricia?" my daughter asks.

She had me thinking.

"I think we both have some growing up to do. It's important to love our friends, to cherish them, and to be committed to them. Girls and women are good at that—and it's a beautiful side to our friendships. But we need to learn to be dependent, leaning on God, because He's the only one who will never betray us or die or move away."[2]

(Kathy) Now I know this was a great lesson, but really—can you believe Dee was concerned that her eight-year-old was codependent?

(Dee) I wasn't actually talking to my eight-year-old about *codependency,* but since Kathy brought it up—let's do! One day Kathy and I were talking about how important our friends were to us, and she said, sort of tongue in cheek, "I think all my friendships are codependent."

We laughed, as I understood that she was simply expressing her great love and need for her friends. But then I said: "Oh, Kath. I know your friends. You have healthy friendships, and I really respect the women you love. From what I see, you and your friends help one another find strength in God, rather than in each other."

"You know, Dee, I think Jan Silvious has a great explanation of codependency. She says that one friend, who is weak, needs the friend who is strong. At first it works great, but in time, the strong friend cannot do enough, because only the Lord can meet our deepest needs. The weak friend is angry, the strong friend is hurt and feels controlled by the weak friend's needs. The friendship is no longer working."

Codependency is a term that people toss about with lots of definitions, but at the root is a false expectation that someone can be to us what only God can be. This error can be destructive in both marriage and in friendship.

Both of us have counseled women who are afraid to separate from abusive or addicted husbands. They say things like:

"What if I lose him?"

"How will I support myself?"

"How can I leave him when he needs me so much?"

So they stay, putting up with the pain, sometimes for a lifetime. That's an understandable choice, but it is not a choice of strength or faith. To really help him, to gain hope for a healthy marriage, the woman must draw boundaries.

We have also seen women make a different choice, a courageous one: they go to their families, local churches, or shelters for help. We have seen God come through for them. Sometimes this decision also causes their husbands to get counseling, turn to God, and to get well; other times, it is only the women who turn to God. But then there is at least *hope* for the husbands. Often it takes a tough love that requires separation to bring another to his senses. And this is exactly what the Lord did in the book of Hosea for His unfaithful bride.

God designed marriage, because of the sexual relationship, for exclusivity. God never intended friendship to be exclusive. When a friend is often upset because you spend time with other people or feels hurt if you are not readily available, you have become an idol to her. Again, the root problem is that she has the false expectation that you can be what only God can be.

Friendship, when it is pure, is a wonderful gift God designed to help us find strength in Him. Spiritually healthy people understand the limitations of friendship and do not expect friends to be all things to them. Because healthy people have their deepest needs met by God, they hold their earthly friends with open hands and welcome others into the friendship circle.

(*Kathy*) Allyson was my closest friend when I was at my lowest in the 1980s. I was not a pretty sight, and yet she was my confidante, counselor, and cheerleader when we were both in Nashville. But then she moved to Colorado, where she began to study counseling and to date her future husband. I moved back to New York and was dealing with my mother's terminal illness. It was then that I met Ellie. We had an instant rapport. Ellie and I wanted to spend time together, but I was so consumed with my mother's illness.

So often friendships escalate in the midst of a trying situation. There I was in New York City with my sick mom, feeling confused and lonely. I was in the waiting room looking out at a wet, dreary day. Feeling chilled, I decided to get a cup of coffee. As I was turning the corner, I ran into Ellie. She was a little out of breath, holding her soggy umbrella. I was shocked, yet elated. "What are you doing here?" She lived fifty miles away.

"I told Frank I needed to be here with you."

I wanted to sob. Our friendship became the kind of balm to my soul that I'd known only with Allyson. It was obvious over the next year that Ellie was becoming dear to me, especially to Allyson. It wouldn't have been like us not to talk about it, not to address it.

Although Allyson felt what any of us would feel—a sense of loss—her response was one of the greatest gifts she ever gave me. She said, "Kath, I can only want God's best for you. I want what He wants for you. Ellie has brought you a sense of family, belonging, and solace. Why wouldn't I want that for you? I love you."

STANDING IN THE GAP

(Dee) I love Kathy's story because it shows that we can be very close to someone and yet have a completely healthy friendship. Sometimes one is weak while the other is strong. But the One who is always strong is Jesus, and we must help one another find strength in Him. If your dependence is on the Jesus *inside* your friend (or spouse), then, if God removes that friend or spouse, you will survive. When that kind of friendship happens, it is a beautiful gift.

Kathy and I have been blessed in working together, but we also have been blessed in our friendship. Sometimes I have been the strong one, and sometimes I have sobbed in her arms. Recently we went to a Women of Faith conference where a number of Christian women speakers and singers share. There Babbie Mason sang a love song to her husband called "After All These Years." Because of Steve's cancer, I began to sob. Kathy had been sitting two seats down, next to her dear friend Valerie, but one look at me and she was scrambling to change seats with Valerie. She held me and I put my head on her shoulder, weeping. Then Babbie began to sing "Standing in the Gap for You," and Kathy sang it over me.

I'll be standing in the gap for you.
Just remember somewhere someone is praying for you,
Calling out your name, praying for your strength.
I'll be standing in the gap for you.[3]

As I thought about that, I was so thankful for the health in our friendship. It's good, it's pure, and it's centered in God.

If our own relationship with God is healthy, if He is first in our lives, then quite naturally, we will help our friends find strength in Him. If God is not first in our lives, then we, especially as women, will tend to make people our gods. If we are idolaters with people, the Lord may need to unclasp our fingers.

When I went through a temporary emotional estrangement with our adult daughter Sally, the Lord had my full attention. I repented continually of everything I could think of, constantly searching my soul. I sensed I had held my daughter too tightly, adored her too much, and been too involved in trying to "fix" her life. I felt the Lord was unclasping my hands, asking me to trust Him with my daughter and to allow Him to be first in my affections. Truly, I was able to abandon Sally to the arms of God.

After I did, the Lord spoke tenderly to me, and, in His time, brought my daughter and me closer than ever. (In fact, she has left the San Francisco Art Institute to come home and live with us right now, during her dad's illness.) Had I not let Sally go, I doubt that our relationship would be as sweet as it is today, and I know I wouldn't be where I am with God. The Lord can't fill our hands when they are clutching something else.

This is why sometimes He has to allure us into the wilderness, away from all the people and the things we tend to clutch so tightly.

There are going to be times in each of our lives when we realize the only One who can truly help us is God. Author Beth Moore has said that Jesus had a large circle of friends (the twelve disciples), an intimate circle (Peter, James, John) and finally, there were times, as in Gethsemane, when He had only His Father. How beautifully this was illustrated in the movie *The Passion of the Christ*.

Sometimes only God will be there for us. If we don't understand this, God may have to show us, by taking us alone into the wilderness. It is only then that we can discover a whole different devotion toward the only One who will never fail us.

Spurgeon put it like this:

> "I will allure her to myself," and then, "I will take her into the wilderness, she shall be in my company, and in nobody else's company." That is just what the grace of God does. She had forgotten him before, but now . . . instead of not thinking of him at all, he is in the first thoughts of the morning, and in the thoughts all day long.[4]

You Are My Hiding Place

When we are going through a valley of trouble, we must run into His arms, bury our heads in His chest, surrender all our brokenness, and allow His strength, words, and healing power to flow into us. Kathy often tells women, "Don't despise the circumstance you are in. It may be the very thing He is using to draw you to Him and to bring comfort to others in the future."

There is such a sweet promise in Hosea 2:14: He will "speak comfort" to us. This phrase appears in Scripture when men spoke tenderly to women, as when Boaz was so kind to Ruth, and she fell down before him, saying, "You have comforted me, and have spoken kindly to your maidservant" (Ruth 2:13). Boaz protected Ruth, provided for Ruth, spoke tenderly to her, and he became, truly, a picture of Jesus.

When we are in the wilderness, for whatever reason, it is vital that we run to Jesus—and He will "speak tenderly" to us.

(Kathy) I often speak about moving to Nashville in my early twenties. I was lonely, in culture shock, and wondering if I really was going to get that chance to record. It was the first time in my life I started journaling. So much was going on in my heart that it all came out in prayers and cries to Jesus.

I'm amazed now as I look through some of the stacks of journals from that time. God has been so faithful to answer some of those heart cries. He really does hear the cries of the brokenhearted. And I guess as I've grown older, I've seen more and more that God does everything in His own timing. I prayed those prayers in the early 1980s, and He is answering some of them just now.

Not only will He speak tenderly to us, He tells us that "the Valley of Achor" will be a "door of hope" (v. 15). He will restore our vineyards, our joy, our singing. Weeping lasts for the night, but "joy comes in the morning" (Psalm 30:5). That is a promise to every believer.

COME, HOLY SPIRIT

The joy that comes in the morning is a result of God's gift of the Holy Spirit welling up in our hearts. This person of the Godhead, living in us, makes it possible for us, in our depravity, to love Him. Hosea looked forward to such a time when he said,

> *"And it shall be, in that day,"*
> *Says the LORD,*

> *"That you will call Me 'My Husband,'*
> *And no longer call Me 'My Master.'"*
>
> —HOSEA 2:16

The word for "husband" here is a tender one: *ishi*. God permits believers some warm names such as *Abba* ("Dearest Father") and *ishi*. Here, in Hosea, more is going on, for the Hebrew word for "Master" (*ba'li*) sounds a lot like "Baal," the false god the Israelites had worshiped. So calling the Lord a name that sounded like "Baal" was very hurtful to Him. It would be like an adulterous wife whose husband has forgiven her, whispering the name of her lover in their marriage bed.

But we should realize that the Lord is equipping us *now*, on earth, to experience more power, more purity, and more of His presence. We live in the time of the new covenant. You see, in Hosea's day, God's bride had been unable to keep the Law. Though the Law was holy and good, she could not live up to it. So the Lord promised a new covenant, when He would write His law on her heart, when He would put His Spirit within her, when He would betroth to her the qualities she so desperately needed to be a pure and holy bride. The scene in the divorce court was over. He had courted her again, alluring her, winning her heart. Now He was going to betroth her again.

Betrothal, in biblical days, was as binding as marriage. Though the marriage had not been consummated, a betrothed woman was considered a wife. A bridegroom gave a bride price as a "down payment" to show that his intentions were sure. What bride price has Jesus given for us? What "down payment"? His blood and His Spirit. His blood cleanses, and His Spirit empowers. Through His Spirit He will protect, love, and show kindness to us, for that is His character. But— and this is the exciting part—He is also going to implant, to sow in our hearts, those qualities that will enable us to keep our part of the covenant! J. B. Phillips version paraphrases this passage as follows:

> I will take you to be my wife for ever.
> I will take you to be my wife rightly and justly,
> I will take you in kindness and mercy.
> I will take you to be my wife in faithfulness,
> And you shall know the Lord.
>
> —HOSEA 2:19–20 PHILLIPS

Notice how the Lord repeats "I will take you" four times, or, in other translations, three times, "I will betroth you." Derek Kidner writes,

> Coming three times in quick succession, the word "betroth" gives a note of eagerness and warmth to what is promised. It makes a new beginning, with all the freshness of first love, rather than the weary patching up of difference—and this is appropriate, since a new covenant brings with it new life.[5]

God is looking forward to a day when the names of our adulterous lovers are truly out of our mouths, when we run to Him and Him alone. We are in process and learning to do so, but we still, on earth, fight with our old natures. One day, and what a day that will be, the struggle will be over, and our natures will be completely changed. Charles Spurgeon wrote,

> Oh! what a blessed thought; the name of Baalim out of my mouth, sin out of my heart, the lustful glance from my

eye, evil things from my imagination, all gone! Oh! will we not praise our Lord in the bright moment when we wake up in his likeness, when our glorified spirit shall be white as driven snow, in the glad companionship of the immaculate, the pure, the perfect? Oh, what joyous shouts we shall raise then! What choral symphonies, what bursts of song, what hallelujahs of gratitude![6]

I Am His, and He Is Mine

The betrothal scene continues at the close of Hosea 2, moving into an actual wedding where the Lord took Israel as His bride, and she took Him as her Husband. The land that He had once judged and made barren was now planted and made fruitful. It's a beautiful and central picture, and one that is being fulfilled right now under the promise of the new covenant. The chapter closes with these covenant words, which are repeated elsewhere in Scripture because they are crucial:

> And I will have mercy on her who had not obtained mercy;
> Then I will say to those who were not My people,
> "You are My People!"
> And they shall say, "You are my God!"
>
> —HOSEA 2:23

It is vital to see that this closing verse in Hosea 2 is the mystery that is revealed in the New Testament. As R. C. Sproul says, this "passage went unnoticed by the vast majority of people for centuries and centuries and centuries. . . . The prophetic utterance here was veiled and cloaked in mystery."

Do you realize that those of you who are Gentiles have no original intrinsic claim to the Kingdom of God? Salvation is to the Jews. Israel is the chosen nation. We had no inheritance. . . . You were nothing. No people. And God has said to you, "Ammi [my people]." That is the mystery of mysteries. Through the irony of the very sin of Israel, that where their wickedness abounded, God's grace abounded. Through their prostitution, you were invited to the wedding. . . . Hardness in part has happened to Israel that the time of the Gentiles should happen. And I for one see hope in this passage for an even greater restoration for the original children of the covenant.[7]

(Dee) My pastor, Mike Lano, explains that the primary purpose of Sunday worship is not evangelism, teaching, or even praise—though those elements should be parts of the service. The purpose of Sunday worship is a renewal of our covenant with God. Every week, because of our bent toward sin, our tendency to be unfaithful brides, we need to come to Him in confession. We will find Him eager to renew the covenant.

Consider seeing your worship service as a dialogue in which you renew your covenant. Let me show you what I mean through our typical order of worship on the next page.

The order of worship at your church may be slightly different, but think about it, and see if you can identify a similar dialogue.

Not only on Sundays, but every day, every time we move out of the light, we need a renewal of covenant. We are weak, but He is so eager to forgive the contrite heart and to run to our sides and strengthen us to be beautiful brides.

Order of Worship	Explanation	Dialogue
Call to worship	Music played	You are my people!
Confession of sin	Scriptural prayer by people	You are my God!
Promise of forgiveness	Scripture promise read by elder	You are my people!
Hymns and choruses	Expressing thanks and love	You are my God!
The Scripture passage read	Word from God	You are my people!
Offering	Expressing love	You are my God!
The Word is expounded	Word from God	You are my people!
Hymn of response	"Bear Fruit, O Word from Heaven"	You are my God!
Benediction	His promise to be with us	You are my people!

Perhaps the clearest picture of God's steadfast love is in the picture of Hosea and Gomer. She absolutely broke his heart, but Hosea kept loving her. Even after he had been so kind to her and she had run back to her former lover, he sought her again and bought her again.

Wherever you are, whatever you've done, He longs for you to let Him be your Redeemer. Oh, how He loves you.

THE REDEEMER

The Redeemer
Artist: Martin French (www.MartinFrench.com)

We opened our house for a Bible study. . . . We eventually came to the book of Hosea . . . that portion of God's Word hit me so profoundly. . . . There are many who struggle to survive in life, many who have been used and abused in the name of love, many who have been sacrificed on the altars of pleasure and "freedom." But the freedom the world offers is, in reality, false. Too many have awakened one day to discover they are in bondage, and they have no idea how to escape it. It is for people such as these that I wrote Redeeming Love.

—FRANCINE RIVERS

7

The Redeemer

Dee) I have watched in awe as Jesus has acted as Redeemer to our daughter Beth, whom we adopted at the age of twelve from Thailand. Abused and abandoned as a baby on the streets of Bangkok, she was found and taken to the hospital. She then spent the first twelve years of her life in an orphanage where she experienced more abuse. Not only did some emotionally sick adults care for her, but the children, who were all handicapped in some way, developed a lifestyle of picking on each other—much the way you see happening in a prison, where hurt people hurt people. Yet God heard her cry.

I have often told of how my husband and I prayed about the decision to adopt and how, during prayer, my husband clearly heard "a girl who was crying." That girl was Beth, and we flew to her orphanage in Thailand to bring her back as our daughter.

As Beth's mother, I am astounded at the number of wonderful godly people God has provided for her: friends, mentors, and counselors. I have a dear friend who offered to have Beth come to her house daily to learn English. Jan tutored Beth for three years, pouring love and life into her. The Lord provided some unusually mature teenage girls to love Beth in her high school years. Right now a devout young woman is mentoring Beth, working through Dan Allender's *The Wounded Heart* with her, helping her resolve deep hurts from the past.

Beth graduates this year and wants to move to a bigger city to pursue a career. Recently my daughter-in-law said, "Please have her move to Kansas City and live with us. John can build her a little apartment downstairs, and she can stay as long as she wants!" I have often said to Beth, "Do you see it, honey? Wherever you turn, God is sending someone to help you! He surely loves you." She nods, her dark eyes shining.

AMAZING GRACE

Recently Beth received an assignment at the University of Nebraska to bring a song or poem and give a short speech on why it was meaningful to her. She brought a medley of songs sung by Point of Grace, all focused on the grace of God. I know she stunned the class. They weren't expecting this painfully shy beauty to share so openly and honestly. Because Beth was twelve when she began to learn English, and because Thai is so different from English, she still struggles with an accent and with grammar.

She certainly didn't lead into her story gently, for she began, ""I lost my arm when I a baby. They left me. But I not die. Somebody found me."

Then Beth pushed Play on the tape recorder, and the class heard,

Who am I that You would love me so gently?
Who am I that You would recognize my name?
Lord, who am I that You would speak to me so softly?
Conversation with the Lord most high, who am I?

She continued, "In the orphanage in Thailand, I have no place to belong. People hurt me and I, myself, hurt people. But somebody care and brought me to America. Now I belong in a family."

Amazing grace, how sweet the sound that saved a wretch like me,
I once was lost but now I'm found,
Was blind but now I see.
And the more I sing that sweet old song,
The more I understand that I do not comprehend
This love that's coming from your hand.

Then Beth went on, "It still taking me awhile to realize that someone love me enough to draw me out of my darkness. Not knowing what the futures may have in store for me. But I am glad to find someone who loves me as I am."

Who am I that You would love me so gently?
Who am I that You would recognize my name?
Lord, who am I that You would speak to me so softly?
Conversation with the Lord most high, who am I?[1]

As she concluded her talk, people were visibly weeping, as she said, "I struggle with hurts in my heart. I struggle with bad habits. But God care. God sending people who care about me just as I am, care about my hurts, care about helping me find another life."

Grace, grace, God's grace,
Grace that will pardon and cleanse within;
Grace, grace, God's grace,
Grace that is greater than all our sin.

We have a Redeemer who longs to rescue us from our chains. No matter our darkness, His light is brighter. No matter the price for our chains, He will pay it. No matter how deep our pit, His arm is longer. No matter where we go, He will be there.

I Know That My Redeemer Lives

Long before Hosea, long before Ruth, lived a righteous man named Job. Satan felt that Job trusted God because God had protected Job with a hedge. Satan wanted God to remove the hedge. Even after Job's children had all died in a disaster, Job still trusted God. Then Satan pressed further, convinced that if Job *himself* were afflicted, if his skin broke out in boils, then he would curse God. Yet even when his flesh was oozing with sores, Job clung to God. He longed to leave a legacy honoring God. In answer to his prayer, Job is momentarily lifted out of his despair and rocketed into a kind of prophetic ecstasy where he "utters mysteries with his spirit" (1 Corinthians 14:2 NIV). The entire book rises to an amazing climax here, a climax centering on this mysterious, thrilling word *Redeemer.*[2]

He proclaimed the words that have gone down in history, that have indeed left him a legacy. They are amazing, for in 1500 BC, Job had a vision of the return of Christ: that magnificent day when the dead in Christ will rise, and in exchange for their decayed flesh and decomposed bodies they will receive strong, healthy bodies. And they will see their Redeemer, face to face, standing upon the earth.

For I know that my Redeemer lives,
And He shall stand at last on the earth;
And after my skin is destroyed, this I know,
That in my flesh I shall see God,
Whom I shall see for myself,
And my eyes shall behold, and not another.
How my heart yearns within me!

—JOB 19:25–27

Mike Mason describes what this word *go'el* (redeemer) meant to Jewish ears:

> It was a delicious word, a passionate word, a word that smacked of chains falling off, of finding buried treasure, of suddenly having more good fortune fall into one's lap than one had ever dreamed or imagined.[3]

Mason, in *The Gospel According to Job*, comments that the word *go'el* "happens to come remarkably close to another word that can ignite our hearts: Gospel." He goes on to explain:

> In Hebrew the word is *go'el*, and it had two general applications. In daily usage its primary meaning was "one who restores," or "one who puts something back into its original or pristine condition." For Christians who know the Lord not only as their Creator but as their re-Creator, this primary meaning of the word *go'el* is rich in connotation.[4]

(*Kathy*) When I left Christian music in the mid-1980s and moved back to New York, I was introduced to a beautiful, godly Catholic woman named Ellen Comis. Although she held big meetings involving healing and great teaching, I was blessed enough to get some precious times alone in conversation with her. I hear she's still in ministry to this day, and it warms my heart. I don't think this woman has any idea how much my thoughts go back to that time in my life that was so painful.

Back then, I carried around so much confusion, self-contempt, and shame. I was also disillusioned by the hypocrisy in the church. But Ellen was real and lovely, and my encounters with her always pointed me to Jesus. One thing that I often imagined for myself and even prayed for hundreds of times—by faith, because I didn't think it was possible—was that I could one day be as comfortable in my skin, be as classy and radiant and as stylish and womanly as she was.

(Dee) It's hard for me to imagine a time when Kathy had so much self-contempt and felt so unsure of herself. Anyone who knows her now sees such a beautiful woman. Because she once had so much "body shame," because she was in the throes of a food addiction, she still gets a kick out of women asking her where she gets her clothes. Kathy has also been transformed on the inside: she has poise, grace, and radiance.

Recently I heard a woman tell her after a conference, "You have the most stunning spirit I have ever seen in a person." I saw what a gift those words were to Kathy as I know, for years, she has prayed for the Spirit of God to transform her character. This is how redemption works: as we press in close to the Redeemer, He will "re-create" us. How He longs to honor those prayers that plead for a redemption of our character.

The other application of *go'el* is best illustrated by the stories of Ruth and of Gomer: two women in destitute circumstances who were redeemed by a "Prince Charming," a man who was related to them, who cared about them, and who was willing to pay a price to rescue them.

There Is a Redeemer

In *Falling in Love with Jesus,* we spent a great deal of time in the book of Ruth, and in considering Boaz, the "kinsman-redeemer" who was a picture of Jesus. Mike Mason captures the romance of Ruth when he explains:

> Boaz—this elder, avuncular, bourgeois landowner who, though related to Ruth, has no more reason to take notice of her than to fly to the moon—this man actually falls head over heels in love with a poor and alien peasant girl! . . .
>
> The moral of the story is that this is exactly how our Lord feels toward us. Although there is no reason on earth why the great King of the Universe should look twice at this petty, filthy breed of grasshoppers called mankind, nevertheless He says to us, "You have stolen my heart, my sister, my bride; you have stolen my heart with one glance of your eyes" (Song 4:9). Imagine—we have stolen the heart of God! And this same awesome, awestruck God turns out to be our very own next-of-kin, our long-lost rich relative, the one person who happens to be closer to us than anybody else and who is bound to us inextricably—not only by a blood covenant, but also, astoundingly, by the simple fact of His profoundly genu-ine love for us.[5]

Perhaps you recall the story we shared in *Falling in Love with Jesus* about Dee's friend Jill, a modern-day Ruth who met a modern-day

Boaz. Jill lost her husband in a farming accident and then eventually was unable to keep up the farm and had to move into town. But a few years later a wonderful man named Keith married Jill. Keith (our Boaz) made it possible for Jill and the children to move back to the farm they had known and loved. He filled Jill's longing for a loving husband and godly father for her four young children. Truly, this is the picture of the *go'el* who is a protector of life and property because of love.[6]

(*Kathy*) I've had the pleasure of getting to know Jill because she now works as Dee's manager. I had heard Dee talk about her in our presentations and was always moved by her story. Jill is a "salt of the earth" kind of gal. She is lovely and would do anything for anyone. Lots of times when I call the Brestin home, Jill answers.

One of those times she invited me to come over for dinner at the farm. I told her that I would be delighted. She then went on to tell me that Keith would love to take me out to the fields to show me what he does. I just smiled because I'd finally get to meet Boaz.

The day came, and Jill told Dee that she'd go before us and meet us out in the cornfields where Keith was working. We drove down lots of dirt roads and finally stopped at an endless row of cornstalks. I thought, *We're not fooling around here. This is the real deal.* Before I knew it, I saw this gigantic green machine coming our way. I thought, *What on earth . . .* I was told it was a combine. When it came to a stop, I saw a handsome man in flannel and jeans who had a big smile on his face. He greeted Dee and me with a warm hello. All that kept on going through my mind initially was, *How come I've met so many Bozos? Jesus, send me a Boaz.* Jill interrupted my thought: "Why don't you take a ride with Keith?"

I said, "Sure. I'll get in the columbine, uh . . . concubine—no, no, no, no—I mean combine." I apologized quickly to sweet Boaz.

Before I knew it, I was sitting in the green monster plowing through thousands of cornstalks, watching the machine strip them of their treasure. I was thrilled and asked Keith all kinds of questions. (For a moment I wanted to live on a farm—but I knew I loved Hyatts and Hiltons too much.) All through my time in the cornfields, I kept thinking about planting, sowing, and reaping, and other things God talks about. It will always be a sweet memory.

We got back to the house, and "Ruth" had prepared a lovely dinner for all of us. Boaz sat at the table, fresh and showered, ready to enjoy a feast after a long, hard day's work. It wasn't long before I saw how devoted and how in love Jill and Keith were. It started me asking him many questions about how they met. It was a blind date, and he had told her he was fat, gray, and short. (He's actually very handsome!) As the night came to a close, I was so thankful that I experienced, in the flesh, what God feels for each of us. What an amazing Kinsman-Redeemer we have.

The portrait of Boaz rescuing Ruth as her *go'el* is similar to the portrait of Hosea rescuing Gomer. Walter Wangerin, in *The Book of God: The Bible as a Novel,* tells the story like this:

> There was in Israel a prophet named Hosea who married a woman named Gomer. In the early years of their marriage she bore her husband three children. . . . But after they had grown into stout youths, Gomer suddenly gathered her things and ran away from her house, her husband, and her family.
>
> She took a lover. She descended into harlotry. Soon she was possessed by another man as a slave is possessed by a master.
>
> . . . And to Hosea himself, the Lord said: "Go again

and love the woman who has become an adulterer with another man. Love her, Hosea, even as I the Lord love the people of Israel, though they have turned to other gods."

So Hosea bought his wife back again for fifteen shekels of silver and a measure of barley.

And he said to her, "You must live faithfully to me. You cannot belong to another man anymore. And I will be faithful to you."

So he took her back again and loved her.

. . . O Israel! I will betroth you to me in righteousness and justice, in steadfast love and in mercy.

For I have pity on Not Pitied!

And I say to Not My People, no! You are my people!

Please answer me now. Please say unto me, "You are our God."[7]

My Redeemer Is Faithful and True

Hosea 3 is the intensely personal account, too painful for elaboration, of Hosea "buying back" his adulterous wife. You must read between the lines to see the hurt and humiliation in Hosea and also in Gomer. Her false lover was done with her and was selling her on the slave market. Can you imagine her shame? In chains, naked, exposed—men were looking her over, bidding on her. Her head was bowed when she heard a familiar, gentle voice. *It's Hosea.* She looked up to see the face of the husband she had betrayed.

One of the responsibilities that God gives husbands is to protect and to provide for their wives: to "cover" them. Husbands are a reflection of the Lord and the way He covers His bride. We love the way Martin French has pictured Hosea covering Gomer with his garment.

Gomer's story has similarities to Ruth's, with one important difference: Gomer is the personification of infidelity, whereas Ruth is the personification of fidelity. Yet the Lord loved them both, not because of their character, but because of His. We are fickle, but He is faithful. We are unworthy, but He is worthy.

Up until now we have looked at this story primarily from Hosea's perspective, but it is also important that we understand Gomer's viewpoint. Gomer represents not only unfaithful Israel and the corporate bride of Christ, but also you and me. As Derek Kidner says, "Israel's sin is also humanity's and everyman's."[8] Some of you, like the woman in Francine Rivers's novel *Redeeming Love,* had a hard start in life. Abused and neglected, you found that sin in the world made you its prisoner. But even those of us who were blessed with loving Christian parents have experienced the slavery of sin. Jesus said,

> *Most assuredly, I say to you, whoever commits sin is a slave of sin.*
>
> —JOHN 8:34

We have all been deceived, lured into a trap. The lovers we thought would comfort us have turned on us. We all need to be freed from our chains. A price had to be paid by someone who cared enough to do that. Hosea paid with silver and barley, but Jesus paid with His life to set us free.

WORTHY IS THE LAMB

Christ is, indeed, our Redeemer. We told you, in the beginning, that the portraits we saw in Hosea we also saw in John. We have seen this is true in each of the portraits so far, but where is the picture of *The*

Redeemer in John? Remember, a redeemer pays a price to set someone free. Hosea paid with a few coins and a few bushels of barley to redeem his wife. James Montgomery Boice parallels our situation with Gomer's:

> We are the slave sold on the auction block of sin. . . . But when all seemed lost, God sent the Lord Jesus Christ, his Son, into the marketplace to buy us at the close of his life. If you can understand it as an illustration, God was the auctioneer. He said, "What am I bid for these poor, hopeless, enslaved sinners?"
>
> Jesus said, "I bid the price of my blood."
>
> The Father said, "Sold to the Lord Jesus Christ for the price of his blood." There was no greater bid than that.
>
> So we became his, and he took us and clothed us, not with the dirty robes of our old unrighteousnesses, which are as filthy rags, but with the robes of his righteousness.[9]

Jesus is called "the Lamb of God" because He was sacrificed for our sin, like the lambs in the Old Testament. The very *first* time Jesus appeared on the scene in the Gospel of John, John the Baptist said:

> *Behold! The Lamb of God who takes away the sin of the world!*
> —JOHN 1:29

We are called the bride of the Lamb (see Revelation 21:9). We were redeemed, Peter explained,

> *with the precious blood of Christ, as of a lamb without blemish*

and without spot. He indeed was foreordained before the foun-
dation of the world.

—1 Peter 1:19–20

Isn't it amazing that God planned for Jesus to be the Lamb "before the foundation of the world"? He even planned the exact moment it would happen. It is not coincidence that the first Easter coincided with Passover. As the lambs were being slaughtered, according to Passover law, our perfect Lamb of God walked the streets of the Via Dolorosa to be slain. Darrell Bock explains several parallels:

> Jesus' condemnation occurs at noon on the day before the Passover (19:14), at the very time the priests were beginning to slaughter the Passover lambs in the temple.
>
> While he was on the cross, "hyssop" was used to give Jesus a sponge of wine (19:29), and hyssop was also used to smear the blood of the Passover lamb on the doorposts in Exodus 12:22.
>
> Furthermore, John 19:36 sees a fulfillment of Scripture in that none of Jesus' bones were broken, and according to Exodus 12:46 no bone of the Passover lamb was to be broken.[10]

(Dee) Imagine yourself back in the days of the first Passover. (I have read many sermons by Charles Spurgeon on this passage, and he has helped me relive the event.) What a night of terror and wonder! The sun is setting and your husband brings in a lamb, a male in his prime who must be without blemish. You all watch him intently, sensing his solemnity as he checks the lamb with great care. He tells your eldest son to get a basin to collect the blood when he stabs the lamb with a knife. He takes a thick branch of hyssop and dips it in the basin of blood. When he smears it over and on either side of the door, your youngest asks, "Why are you doing this, Father? What does this mean?"

He replies, "This is a clear sign for the Lord to see. Tonight the angel of death will come and strike—but do not fear, for we are safe. We are under the blood of the lamb." You prepare the Passover meal, roasting the lamb, taking pains not to break any bones. Your family sits down to the meal: the lamb, the unleavened bread, and the bitter herbs. Your husband gives a blessing, his voice filled with gratitude and emotion.

When he looks up, joy is in his face. "We will not work as slaves tomorrow. Son, you will not feel that whip on your back ever again. Daughter, you will never be abused by our cruel taskmaster. My darling wife, we will all soon be free!"

You are dressed to flee, with sandals, a pack of clothes on your back, and a walking stick. Suddenly a shriek pierces the still night. Then another. Soon you hear weeping and wailing everywhere outside. The Egyptians come, pounding on your door, *pleading* with you to leave. A mother is cradling the body of her son in her arms. The grieving father says: "If you do not leave, we shall all be dead!" It is still dark, but you leave quickly, joining the thousands of Israelites in exodus.

How thankful we are that Jesus is our perfect Lamb, whose blood has caused the wrath of God to pass over us. He is our hiding place.

YOU ARE MY HIDING PLACE

(*Dee*) For many years I thought the way to overcome the power of sin was to read my Bible more, pray more, and so on. The problem with my thinking was that though those disciplines are critical to my spiritual health, I was still trusting that *I* could do it—and you know what? *I* can't. I can't overcome the power of sin any more than I can overcome the penalty of sin. It has to be Jesus.

So, what is the solution? There's a story in *Prince Caspian,* from C. S. Lewis's Narnia series, that gives insight. The great lion, Aslan (who represents Jesus), has asked a young girl named Lucy to do something difficult:

> "Do you mean that is what you want me to do?" gasped Lucy.
>
> ". . . It is hard for you, little one," said Aslan. . . .
>
> Lucy buried her head in his mane to hide from his face. But there must have been some magic in his mane. She could feel lion-strength going into her. Quite suddenly she sat up.
>
> "I'm sorry, Aslan," she said, "I'm ready now.
>
> "Now you are a lioness," said Aslan.[11]

Do you see? The secret isn't in what I can do, but in what the mighty power of Christ can do through me. The reason we are so excited about the whole concept of falling in love with Jesus is that our love relationship is the key to strength. We must bury our faces in his mane and keep them there until we sense "lion-strength" going into us. Surely, spending time with Him in His Word and in prayer does deepen our love relationship with Him, but it's a critical difference to remember to rely on His power instead of our own. When we bury our faces in His mane, when we are still, and know that He is God, He reminds us of His love and gives us the faith to submit, not to the flesh, but to the Spirit. Each time we do that, more "lion-strength" grows in us, helping us defeat the old nature.

Redemption from the power of sin will not be complete until we see Jesus face to face with our new, sanctified bodies. But, through faith, we can see the new nature grow stronger and the old nature weaker. John Calvin tells us not to despond because we have not wholly crucified the flesh:

> For this work of God is not completed in the day in which it is begun in us; but it gradually goes on, and by daily advances is brought by degrees to its end.[12]

We have just considered Jesus as the Lamb of God. This Lamb is not always gentle. In Revelation, John saw in a vision men pleading with the mountains to fall on them to hide them from "the wrath of the Lamb!" (Revelation 6:16). Just as the Lamb is hidden in the Lion, the Lion is hidden in the Lamb.

THE LION

The Lion
Artist: Martin French (www.martinfrench.com)

So I will be to them like a lion;

Like a leopard by the road I will lurk;

I will meet them like a bear deprived of her cubs;

I will tear open their rib cage,

and there I will devour them like a lion.

The wild beast shall tear them.

—HOSEA 13:7–8

8

The Lion

*Y*ou are not likely to find Hosea 13:7–8 crocheted on a cushion or painted on a plaque. The verses we like to display are the ones about His unfailing love, His mercy, and His care.

Likewise, we are drawn to the portraits of the Lord that show His gentle side: a Bridegroom betrothing His bride, a Father teaching His child to walk, and a Redeemer rescuing us. But unless we *also* see the portraits of Jesus that show His holiness and just wrath, we are living in a fantasy world and will fail to mature as we so desperately need to mature. After speaking about the great sin of turning away from the Lord, the author of Hebrews warned us to "serve God acceptably with reverence and godly fear" (Hebrews 12:28) Why? Because, he wrote,

Our God is a consuming fire.

—HEBREWS 12:29

The first principle of the wisdom literature of the Bible is that the fear of the Lord is the beginning of wisdom. But often, after He relieves our fears of hell, we may move into a time, in our immaturity, when we fail to revere Him as we ought. In *Your God Is Too Small,* J. B. Phillips says that we want to reduce God so that we can control Him, making Him a policeman or an indulgent grandfather. But the God of the universe cannot be contained. Even after He has removed our fears of hell, we need to fear dishonoring His name.

(*Dee*) T. S. Eliot called Jesus "Christ the Tiger." And the Irish poet W. B. Yeats wrote, in "The Second Coming," of a lion "slouching" toward us, "moving its slow thighs." I wrote an essay on "The Second Coming" as a student at college, but because I was blind to spiritual truths, I had *no* idea what Yeats was talking about. Apparently my professor didn't either, for I received an A on my senseless essay. (It makes me laugh to think about it now.) In our society, most people are spiritual but blind to the spiritual truths of the gospel of Christ. And even believers often overlook just how holy God is.

Sometimes I wonder how our almighty God feels about the flippant bumper stickers, gaudy T-shirts, and trite trinkets in the marketplace that bear His holy name. (Or how the person wearing the T-shirt or bearing the bumper sticker may disgrace Him with his or her behavior.) Because He is a God of grace, when we make choices that lack reverence, He doesn't routinely cut us down with bolts of lightning but allows us to mature and to understand His majesty and holiness. Kathy told me a story about herself as a new Christian that I am so thankful she, in her typical vulnerability, is willing to tell.

(*Kathy*) I was a very young believer in Jesus when I started singing about Him. Because of the new and exciting thrill of knowing Him and being loved by Him, songs were just pouring out of me. I wasn't an accomplished guitar player and pianist, but with the few chords I knew on both of those instruments, I wrote a lot. This was a season that I was taking in so much I couldn't help but let it out.

I was such a novice at songwriting that the songs were either epics that told His story from Genesis to Revelation (in one song), or quite cute, lighthearted, and playful. Nonetheless, people seemed to enjoy them, and I enjoyed singing them.

I remember reading a little poem comparing God to commercial slogans. I thought it would be fun to put it to music. It ended up having three chords and a title of "God Is Like Pepsi." (Hang in there with me—I'll explain.) I'm probably dating myself, but some of you may remember . . .

> God is like Ford
> He has the better idea
> God is like Coke
> He is the real thing
> God is like Pan Am
> He makes the going great
> God is like Right Guard
> So why should you sweat it?
>
> God is like Pepsi
> He's got a lot to give
> for He sent His only Son
> so that you and I could live.

When I sang at coffeehouses and churches where I'd been before, people screamed out, "Sing the Pepsi song!" (My audiences apparently lacked maturity as well!)

Then I was asked to sing at an Episcopal church in Connecticut.

I remember really enjoying the service. A visiting pastor from Romania gave the message. It was powerful and poignant. I sang through my usual set and again got great laughter and applause from the "Pepsi generation." At the end of the service, through all the hubbub of meeting and greeting, the missionary gently tapped me on the shoulder and asked if he could speak to me. I was anticipating a response like the ones I was getting from others—something like:

"You were wonderful."

"You are so gifted."

"You really blessed me."

"God's going to take you places."

The missionary looked in my eyes intently. What came out of his mouth has stayed with me since that day. It has also deeply affected my awareness of the holiness of God and the call on His people.

"Miss Troccoli, where I am living and ministering, there is great suffering. There are deep cries of prayer to the Father and a holding on to His promises for their very lives. I cannot see my people dying for a God that is like Dial soap."

I was shocked, to say the least. But the missionary's rebuke was so full of the truth. In no way could I refute it, ignore it, or deny it. I never sang the song again.

Many of the portraits painted of Jesus show Him as gentle and mild—even effeminate, as if the artist wanted to strip Him of His power, His holy and righteous indignation, and His strength. Others have claimed that the God of the Old Testament is full of wrath, but the God of the New Testament is gentle and mild. Not so. "Jesus Christ is the same yesterday, today, and forever" (Hebrews 13:8). The anger we see in Hosea is the same anger we see when He overturns the tables of the money changers in John. He does not want us to forget Him or to fail to fear Him. He has been, is now, and will be seeking true worshipers who love Him with all their hearts, souls, and minds.

I Love an Untame Lion

Seizing the heavy tables filled with coins, overturning them on the stone floor, slashing a whip through the air, Jesus terrified the crowd. Tables fell, coins clattered, lambs bleated, birds squawked, and people cried out. John described the scene:

> Now the Passover of the Jews was at hand, and Jesus went up to Jerusalem. And He found in the temple those who sold oxen and sheep and doves, and the money changers doing business. When He had made a whip of cords, He drove them all out of the temple, with the sheep and the oxen, and poured out the changers' money and overturned the tables.
>
> —JOHN 2:13–15

This was the first time Jesus cleared the temple, during a Passover early in His ministry. John's primary point, as is typical of his Gospel, is that Jesus *is* God and therefore had the authority to cleanse the courts of the money changers of the noise, of the animals that were wandering into the temple itself and defecating. Jesus was protecting those who longed to worship. It was a bold and astonishing act, and it frightened the crowd. Leon Morris wrote, "It was not so much the physical force as the moral power" that terrified the crowd.[1]

Later, Jesus cleared the temple *again,* and Matthew, Mark, and Luke recorded that cleansing. That time was after His triumphal entry on what we call Palm Sunday. It was the terrible eve of the Passover on which He would offer Himself as the perfect Lamb of God.[2] The first cleansing shocked the religious leaders, but the second sealed their determination to destroy Jesus.[3]

Neither cleansing was an impulsive act. Our Lord's wrath is different from man's. He never "loses it," but He does become angry. As John White points out, Jesus *made* the whip Himself. "His act of enraged violence was premeditated . . . he made a plan and carried it out."[4]

We need to ask ourselves, *What was it that made God so angry in the book of Hosea? In the book of John?* It is interesting, for the sin was similar. In both cases, people had corrupted the worship of a holy God.

Jesus cleared the money changers from the temple because they were preventing God's people from truly worshiping. The noise of braying animals and bargaining money changers corrupted the worship. Those who were turning God's house into a marketplace simply didn't revere God. Though it pleases God when we understand His great love for us and run into His arms, we must never, ever forget that He is holy, awesome, and above all gods. Basically, they had "forgotten" the true God. And is this not often true of us as well?

- It is not hidden from the Lord Almighty when our worship or our ministry is more about glorifying ourselves than glorifying Him.
- It is not a small thing to a holy God when, because we have failed to fear and to love Him, we are grumbling, gossiping, and sowing discord among brothers.

- It is not unnoticed by the Creator of heaven and earth when we, because of our neglect of Him, are running to the gods of worldly pleasures to fill up our souls.

There were certainly great consequences for the people in Hosea's day. Though they said they loved Yahweh, they brought other gods into their beds. They trifled with Him the way an unfaithful woman trifles with her marriage covenant. So the Lord said:

> *I will be like a lion to Ephraim,*
> *And like a young lion to the house of Judah.*
> *I, even I, will tear them and go away;*
> *I will take them away, and no one shall rescue.*
>
> —HOSEA 5:14

A good part of Hosea is about how God, because of the harlotry of His people, was going to allow them to be captured, torn, and ravaged for many, many years. This was no empty threat, for the prophecy of Hosea was fulfilled when the northern kingdom fell in 722 BC and when the Assyrians invaded the southern kingdom in 701 BC.

What is amazing is not that the Lord became like a lion to His people in Hosea, or that Jesus slashed a whip through the crowd in John, but that we don't see displays of His anger more frequently. We can be thankful that our God is slow to anger and abounding in mercy, or none of us would be standing.

As we grow in our understanding of the holiness of God, we also grow in the understanding of our depravity. Dust and dirt may not be noticeable in a darkened room, but when the drapes are open and the light comes streaming in, the dust dances and the dirt defiles what we once thought to be a lovely room. It's the same way with our sin. When we aren't walking closely with the One who is the Light of the World, we may think we are doing fine. But the closer we draw, the more His holy light exposes our sin.

CLEANSE MY HEART, O GOD

One of the characteristics we have come to love about truly godly friends is that they do see their continual need, for they are in the presence of God's light. When Dee's daughter Sally went to Covenant Seminary in St. Louis, she told of how open the other students were about their sin. "So often," Sally said, "I have been to prayer groups where we concentrated on praying for the needs of friends and family members, but at Covenant, I was blown away by the personal vulnerability." There she heard requests like these:

> "I'm so full of pride—I hate it. Pray I will humble myself before God chooses to do it for me!"

> "I get so jealous of students who have more than I do. Pray I will die to that rottenness and that contentment will live."

> "I am so selfish. All through the day, my thoughts are primarily about myself. Pray for me, please."

One pastor suggested that when criticized because of our depravity, we should say, "You don't know the half of it!"

We can be thankful that, again, our God is slow to anger. But we must not let His grace lull us into thinking that we can disregard His holiness or that our sin does not grieve His heart, or that we can relax in our battle. As long as we live in these bodies, we will have a battle with sin. If we do something wrong and nothing happens, we must not conclude that it doesn't matter to God or that we have "gotten away with it."

Human beings have consistently taken advantage of the grace of God. Solomon commented on this in regard to people in the world:

> *Because the sentence against evil deeds is so long in coming, people in general think they can get by with murder.*
>
> *Even though a person sins and gets by with it hundreds of times throughout a long life, I'm still convinced that the good life is reserved for the person who fears God, who lives reverently in his presence, and that the evil person will not experience a "good" life. No matter how many days he lives, they'll all be as flat and colorless as a shadow—because he doesn't fear God.*
>
> —ECCLESIASTES 8:11–13 MSG

But it isn't just people of the world who think they can get away with murder. We as believers can be full of hatred toward our brothers, persistent in sexual immorality, filled with pride, given over to gluttony, or generally apathetic about our love for God. Why? It may be because God has been gracious to us, and we assume He will always forgive us. Scripture warns against assuming upon grace and becoming apathetic. God will not always strive with us. If we continue in sin, soon we will not even be able to hear His promptings (see Proverbs 2:20–22).

Voltaire once said of God, "Forgiveness? That's his job!" A young man who proclaimed repentance as he left his wife for another woman said the same: "God will forgive me—that's what He does." James Montgomery Boice says, "We are never in greater danger than when we assume that he will always forgive us as long as we go through the outward forms of repentance."[5] The Lord is a God of justice, so although, as the Bible says, His understanding is unfathomable and His love is unending, there comes a point when He says, "No more." Many Christians have watched public Christians fall at the hands of the law. It becomes evident that the fall did not happen overnight. It had been years in the making, slowly brewing. The roots of sin grew wider and deeper until God not only cut down the tree in one fell swoop but drew up the roots, leaving them lying on the ground for all to see.

Continually in Hosea we see a contrast between an unholy and "partially" repentant people and a holy God who will indeed carry out His refining process, not "partially," but completely. God says:

> *They do not cry out to me from their hearts*
> *but wail upon their beds.*
>
> —HOSEA 7:14 NIV

How easy to be sorry for the consequences, yet unwilling to do the U-turn.

If we are stubborn about doing the U-turn, God may become the Lion to us and seek us out. Not only is this true of the corporate church, but the Lord also chooses to be the Lion in our individual lives. Because of His great love for us, He may chasten us for our sin. When we think we can hide our sin from Him, He may, as Hosea said repeatedly, stalk us like a lion, tear at our very beings, and cause us to fear Him as we ought. When we are in rebellion, we may hide, but the Lion can always hunt us and find us. We may run, but the Lion can always overtake us. We may ignore His still, small voice, but the Lord will roar until we come trembling back.

Have you ever heard it said that all sin is the same in God's eyes? It simply isn't so. Even Jesus told Pilate, in speaking of Judas, "The one who delivered Me to you has the greater sin" (John 19:11). So where do we get this erroneous teaching? Sometimes we take true statements, but then, like the person who adds two plus two and gets five, leap to a false conclusion. It seems that some have thought,

All sin grieves the heart of God. (True)

All sin deserves the sentence of death, so even if you have never robbed a bank or murdered anyone, you still need a Savior. (True)

Therefore, all sin is the same in God's eyes. (False)

Ken Gire says that since the first commandment is to love the Lord your God with all your heart, soul, and mind, it would make sense that what would grieve the Lord the most is to *not* love Him with all your heart, soul, and mind. Would this not be similar to "forgetting" Him, as the people in Hosea's day did?

Likewise, since the second commandment is to love our neighbor as ourselves, wouldn't it make sense that we grieve the Lord deeply when we don't? I think the list that Solomon made of sins particularly abhorrent to God bears this out:

> *These six things the LORD hates,*
> *Yes, seven are an abomination to Him:*
> *A proud look,*
> *A lying tongue,*
> *Hands that shed innocent blood,*

A heart that devises wicked plans,
Feet that are swift in running to evil,
A false witness who speaks lies,
and one who sows discord among brethren.
                                        —PROVERBS 6:16–19

This list begins with the root sin, pride, which is about resisting God, and continues to things that are all about hurting others culminating in "sow[ing] discord," something we are so guilty of doing. When we see what is really important to God, we are humbled. We often realize we have been legalistic, defining Christianity by a short list of rules, instead of loving Him and loving others.

There is a similarity between Hosea 4 and Romans 1, in which Paul condemned the whole world because "although they knew God, they did not glorify Him" (Romans 1:21) The Gentiles knew God existed because of Creation, yet they *suppressed* the truth about Him so that they could do what they wanted to do.

The Israelites knew more than the Gentiles did, but they, too, *suppressed* that truth, and for the same reason.

When we come to the realization that God really is smarter than we are and has a better plan for our lives than we do, we hunger and thirst for His Word—and that is what sets us free from the deadly sin of pride. When we see God as He really is, humility has to occur.

Being immersed in Scripture is vital, but it is also important to study *entire books* of the Bible instead of selective passages. Though topical Bible studies and sermons (those that select verses on one topic or person in Scripture) definitely have value, if that is all we are studying, then we are treating the Bible like a smorgasbord from which we select only the verses that please the palate.

We must also be willing to allow the Word of God to change the path we are on. English preacher Ian Tait said that those who study the Bible only to gain more information may believe their minds are expanding when, in fact, only their heads are swelling![6] The Word of God is intended to purify us, change us, and make us like Jesus.

A repeated theme in Hosea is that the people cherished "a spirit of harlotry." They thought they had knowledge of God, but they were selective about their knowledge. They were offering sacrifices and having festivals, but their empty displays of piety only angered God more. There is continual tension in Hosea: They were His people, yet they certainly didn't act like His people. They had some knowledge of Him, but they had suppressed whatever they didn't want to know. They were not satisfied with their lives, but instead of repenting to the one true God, they ran to other gods for help. Yet, God is patient and abounding in mercy, so instead of flattening them, He began to chastise them gently.

I Will Be Like a Moth

The Lord said He would begin not as a lion, but as a fluttering moth! He said:

> *I will be to Ephraim like a moth,*
> *And to the house of Judah like rottenness.*
>
> —Hosea 5:12

What does this mean? James Montgomery Boice writes:

First, a moth distracts us or bothers us in a harmless way.
. . . God may be saying that at the beginning of our path
of disobedience he is like that. He distracts us from sin,

bothers us, tries to get us away from it and back to thinking of him once again.

Second, many moths are destructive. . . . Here is a case where we, having resisted the fluttering of the moth, now find it to have gotten into the things we value and to have destroyed them. God says that he will also do that to turn us to him.[7]

I Will Be Like a Lion

When gentle chastisement fails, God finally determines to be like a lion. It breaks His heart, and He seems to vacillate. He knows He needs to do it—He is a Parent who truly loves His offspring. He fondly remembers Israel as "a child" and is overcome with sorrow (Hosea 11:1). He thinks back to how He "taught Ephraim to walk, taking them by their arms" (Hosea 11:3). What a tender picture of a Father's love.

No wonder He cried:

> How can I give you up, Ephraim?
> How can I hand you over, Israel?
>
> —Hosea 11:8

Yet He had to. For God's people, instead of turning to Him, ran to Assyria and Egypt for help. In their pride they had shut their hearts to the one true God. They would never hear His gentle whisper. He had to roar like a lion; He had to allow His own children to be captured, torn, and ravaged. It was the only hope left to Him for a holy nation.

In chapters 5 through 11 of Hosea, a kaleidoscope of pictures portrays the refining judgment of God. (These are the chapters we seldom study—but we must at least do an overview of them.) The Lord is a lion who seizes and tears, a net who falls over a senseless dove, One who releases a flood of water on them. We know that Hosea's terrible prophecies were fulfilled and that God's people suffered enormously at the hands of the Assyrians and other invading armies.

Yet Hosea also saw the light at the end of the tunnel. By the end of Hosea 11, the people were indeed truly repentant. Instead of flitting like a silly dove between Assyria and Egypt for help, they had had their fill of each and were finally going home to the Father.

THE LION KING

We love the movie *The Lion King*. While it is definitely a mixture of Christianity and spirituality (a little nature worship, a little Eastern religion), if you sift out the dross, you are left with some golden gospel pictures.

In the opening scene, the whole animal kingdom is coming to worship the Lion King and his newborn cub—impalas running, elephants thundering, giraffes loping, and birds soaring, all in great excitement. The Lion King stands high on a cliff, the wind blowing his majestic mane, the sun gleaming on him, and all of the animals bow down. Then he proudly holds up his cub, Simba, and the music soars and creation rejoices. It reminds us of the scene in Revelation 5 where the twenty-four elders bow down to the Lamb of God.

The Lion King reigns over whatever the sun touches, except, as he tells his little Simba, that "area of darkness." (Jesus reigns over *all* principalities, for even Satan must get permission from Him.) The Lion King is tough but tender, and fiercely protective of Simba. Simba could easily represent us as God's erring children. Though Simba wanders into the darkness and experiences great trial, he finally runs home to his father. The father allows Simba to roam, and even to be hurt, for his own good, but, in the end, this Lion King will defeat all enemies. As he says reassuringly to Simba: "Nobody messes with your dad."

As Hosea looked ahead to the future, He saw God's people returning to Him. They would return at the sound of His roar, trembling but thankful to be home.

> *"They shall walk after the* LORD.
> *He will roar like a lion.*
> *When He roars,*
> *Then His sons shall come trembling from the west;*
> *They shall come trembling like a bird from Egypt,*
> *Like a dove from the land of Assyria.*
> *And I will let them dwell in their houses,"*
> *Says the* LORD.
>
> —HOSEA 11:10–11

We do not know which homecoming this picture portrays, for often the prophets saw "several mountain peaks": a near fulfillment, but then a later one and often a final, end-times fulfillment. Derek Kidner writes:

> It is not easy to know which stage of history is in mind here: whether some intermediate day of the lion's roar, such as the overthrow of Babylon . . . or the spiritual homecoming of God's "sons" of many nations in the gospel age . . . or again the great turning of the Lord which is predicted in Romans 11. . . . What is certain is that the final event will far surpass our wisest thoughts and wildest expectations.[8]

John described the final events in Revelation, a vision that, though amazing, cannot begin to tell us, in our limited humanity, what that final day will truly be like. What we can understand is that we will be fully reconciled with God, and the prophecy of Hosea will be fulfilled, as John wrote:

> Behold, the tabernacle of God is with men, and He will dwell with them, and they shall be His people. God Himself will be with them and be their God.
>
> —Revelation 21:3

When that day arrives, though we don't understand many things about heaven, we do know that

> God will wipe away every tear from their eyes;
> there shall be no more death, nor sorrow, nor crying.
> There shall be no more pain,
> for the former things have passed away.
>
> —Revelation 21:4

C. S. Lewis describes the final day like this:

Wrong will be right, when Aslan comes in sight,
At the sound of his roar, sorrows will be no more
When he bares his teeth, winter meets its death,
And when he shakes his mane, we shall all have spring again.[9]

For all of us who believe, no matter how difficult our lives may be, there will be *no more* sorrow, there will be *no more* crying, there will be *no more* pain. What hope there is in Jesus.

THE WAY, THE TRUTH, AND THE LIFE

The Way, the Truth, and the Life
Artist: Martin French (www.martinfrench.com)

In the play Our Town, *Emily is allowed to leave heaven and come to earth, invisible, for a day. She watches her loved ones scurrying about and exclaims: "Oh, Earth, you are too wonderful for anyone to realize you." She then asks, "Do any human beings realize life while they live it?—Every, every minute?" The answer she is given: "No. The saints and the poets. Maybe they do—some."*

—THORNTON WILDER

9

The Way, the Truth, and the Life

Kathy) My friend Valerie Clemente had her parents in town recently. Her mom is in her mideighties, and her dad is ninety-three. I love spending time with people of that generation, hearing their wisdom, their take on things, their stories from the past. Her mom used to be a dancer and is so elegant. Her face is delicately regal. Her dad is so feisty. You could tell he must have been a catch when he was younger. He made his living by playing guitar and bass in clubs all around the Northeast.

I knew he would be delighted to sing me some of the old tunes, so I asked Valerie to get out her guitar. Her dad's old hands wrapped around that guitar, forming wonderful jazz chords, and he began to sing. I joined in, and soon Val's mom was singing along with a sweet, wide vibrato. (Picture Katharine Hepburn singing.) They were back

189

in time, and I was right there with them: "You Are My Sunshine," "Down by the Old Mill Stream."

The next day Val told me what a great time her parents had. She told me it was especially wonderful to see her dad come alive again. He'd been depressed, sleeping a lot. That very morning at Val's house he had told her mom he wanted to die. Her reply had been, "Paul, you can't die here. You have to wait until we go home."

We both laughed. As I thought about it more, I said, "You know what, Val? I think Jesus says that to us."

"What do you mean?"

"Well, so often we want to give up. We get tired. We accept that life is just too hard. We live in a slumberlike state—a deadness . . .

"I think the Lord says, 'You can't die here. You have to wait until you go home.'

"And even then, when we go home, it is only a passing away of our mortal bodies. Death to life. But we can't die now. Jesus came that we would have life—and He meant here and now!"

Jesus is the source of life, not only eternally, but right here, right now. But so often we live like "dead men walking" instead of embracing all that is available to us.

We began this book with the portrait *The Great I AM* and will close with *The Great I AM*. This time we will narrow the focus and look at two of the "I AMs" that promise life: particularly *I AM the Way, the Truth, and the Life* and *I AM the Vine*. Both of these pictures are in the gospel of John but also can be seen in Hosea. Embracing these fully is the key to embracing the life Jesus has for us—here and now.

I AM THE WAY

R. C. Sproul says this:

Jesus claims to be the only way. This exclusiveness is contained in this dramatic statement: 'No one comes to the Father, but by me.' That's on a collision course with all of the pluralism that we hear in America.[1]

Sproul remembers an experience he had as a freshman in college. A professor was berating Christians because of their belief that Jesus is the only way to God. Abruptly he turned the spotlight on Sproul and asked, "Sproul—do you think Jesus is the only way to God?"

Sproul squirmed. If he said no, he would be betraying God. If he said yes, everyone would see him as a bigot.

Softly, Sproul said, "Yes."

The professor turned his fury on the young student. "Jesus the only way? How arrogant, how closed-minded, how ridiculous!" The rest of the hour the professor devoted to belittling Sproul. How terrible is this claim of Christ. And yet . . . how wonderful.

At the end of class, as the other students filed out, Sproul sat quietly, asking God for wisdom and composure. Finally, he picked up his books and approached his professor respectfully.

"Sir, do you think Jesus could be one way to God?"

"Well, yes, Jesus could be one way."

"Sir, if you believe Jesus could be one way and therefore began to study His life and His words and found that He claimed to be the only way—what would you do with that?"

"You would have a dilemma—but it's just so arrogant to say that Jesus is the only way."

Softly, but with a heart of gratitude, Sproul responded: "I'm just so glad there is *one* way."

His professor lifted his eyebrows, confused. With emotion, Sproul continued, "When I think of the price God paid—giving up

His only Son, allowing Him to be beaten, mocked, and crucified—all to pay for my sin, I'm overwhelmed. I can't imagine going to God and saying, 'That's not enough. I'd like more options.'"[2]

(*Dee*) How I appreciate Sproul's winsome way of answering one of the hardest objections to Christianity. The enemy has sown so much deceit that it is difficult for people to hear it. I remember as a young woman wondering how Christians could be so "prideful" as to say Jesus was the only way. It can seem unkind to reject everyone else's belief. I remember listening to Paul Little, an evangelist from the 1960s who spoke on college campuses. I attended a liberal Ivy League university that was rampant with "tolerance" toward all religions except Christianity. Little's voice was a unique but intriguing one. He claimed that our "tolerance" was what was truly unkind, for it was akin to being tolerant of those who wanted to jump out of an airplane with a broken parachute.

Only Jesus rose from the dead. Only Jesus is the Way, the Truth, and the Life. Only Jesus has the power to rescue us from destruction.

Another lie the enemy has sown is that all religions are basically the same. Again, not true. Only Christianity embraces the deity of Christ. Only Christianity says we cannot work our way to heaven. There are other huge differences as well. Many religions are violent, abusive of women, and filled with satanic rituals. Those who say all are the same simply haven't done their homework.

The reason Christians can proclaim that Jesus is the only way is because Jesus, and only Jesus, is God. And once again, we proclaim it because He proclaimed it. The early Christians were not called Christians, but "followers of the Way." This is the watershed issue. Jesus and Jesus alone is the Way, the Truth, and the Life.

Some say they do believe in Jesus, but if you listen carefully, you will see they have redefined Him. "Another Jesus" is being preached in different parts of the world. Many of you can find it in your own community or family.

> Jesus is love,
>> but He's not holiness.

> Jesus is grace,
>> but He's grace without standards.

> Jesus is the Way,
>> but He's not the only way.

People preach another Jesus because they need more options. And even believers like to have a lot of exit ramps going to destinations they desire. Yet we must let the words of Scripture penetrate our hearts:

> *A highway shall be there, and a road,*
> *And it shall be called the Highway of Holiness.*
> —ISAIAH 35:8

> *Enter by the narrow gate; for wide is the gate and broad is the way that leads to destruction, and there are many who go in by it. Because narrow is the gate and difficult is the way which leads to life, and there are few who find it.*
> —MATTHEW 7:13–14

The Way, the Truth, and the Life   193

(*Kathy*) The strong convictions I have about the importance of taking the narrow road of truth inspired "Live for the Lord." I sing many of my songs over and over again, so I always try to sing them as if for the first time. That way they won't get stale to me. I also am conscious of looking in people's eyes so that I can communicate the words powerfully and personally. Well, the other night I was pierced so deeply by my very own lyrics:

> We live in a time when people are blind,
> They're not lovers of truth.
> They'll only believe what they touch and see
> And then think I'm a fool.
> My God is love—He also is holy.
> And in Him I'll trust.[3]

I have been absorbing the news on CNN like a sponge. There are Republicans and Democrats. There are war stories and weather catastrophes. There are crimes and critiques. I have been learning so much, though I find myself often so angry and frustrated. It often makes me cry out to God. I listen to what the Right and the Left have to say, but all it makes me want to do is pay closer attention to the ups and downs in my relationship with Jesus. Oh, how I cling to Him. Without His life, without His absolute truths, there are no boundaries or understanding.

Recently I watched Larry King. His guest was Bill Maher, one of the most eloquent and articulate men I have seen in these forums. How often I wonder what these kinds of men would do for the kingdom of God if Jesus had their hearts. Larry asked Bill all sorts of things on all different subjects. It always amazes me that Bill doesn't have to take a breath—he's right there with an answer. And boy, did it all "make sense."

Topics came up: separation of church and state; gay marriages; abortion. As I said before, I can watch these shows with so many severe opinions and get awfully frustrated and sometimes angry, but somehow this particular response from Bill, when Larry asked his opinion on how he felt about gay marriage, sent a shiver up my spine:

> Listen Larry, it's a no-brainer! Talk about religion and how stupid it is—it would not be an issue except for the Bible, except for religion. That's what is so bad about religion. The Bible is the problem![4]

May Jesus have mercy on our souls.

If only people knew who they were really dealing with. They have no idea who they are pointing their fingers at. It's just like Jesus to wait for a time to reveal His justice, power, and righteousness. We saw it when He hung on the cross: everyone mocking Him, as He hung dying, He could have struck men dead in a millisecond. But He didn't—because of love.

Not only is He love, He is wisdom itself. Dallas Willard said, "Jesus is not just nice. He's brilliant." Willard also says that people think of Jesus in some sort of "feathery realm" that has little to do with them.[5] They see Jesus as an ethereal creature dealing with dogma and law, but not real, with life-bursting energy. Yet Jesus said "I AM the Truth," and also that the truth could set us free. That freedom certainly has to do with real life and real issues. His solutions are brilliant.

> The young wife who has a sexually immoral past that haunts her marriage bed—wouldn't she like to be free of the guilt?

The father who, like his father, lashes out in anger. Rage wells up in him, and he loses control—wouldn't he like to be free of the rage?

The obese woman who comforts herself in secret with food but weeps over her body—wouldn't she like to be free of this addiction?

The believer who battles homosexual yearnings and is enslaved in unhealthy relationships—wouldn't she like to be free of this bondage?

The first step in breaking chains is simply to realize that there is such a thing as definable truth. Francis Schaeffer, a twentieth-century theologian, describes in his book *The God Who Is There* a shift in thinking about truth in our world. The belief that there is no definable truth is what Schaeffer calls "the line of despair." This is not a place where people wallow in sadness, but a place where truth cannot be defined. Above the line of despair people can say with conviction, "This is right" or "That can't be true." But below the line, they can no longer recognize truth.

Schaeffer says that Europeans dropped below the line of despair after 1890, and Americans after 1930. Today, whatever you believe is true, and people consider you judgmental to tell someone that premarital sex, homosexuality, abortion, or a multitude of other choices are wrong. As long as there is no definable truth, there is no hope for release from the chains of sin.

That doesn't mean we should barge in and tell someone his lifestyle is wrong. Truly, that is putting the cart before the horse.

First, he must see the love and hope of Jesus, and then he will be intrigued enough to ask questions.

(*Dee*) In our own lives, as we practice the truths of Scripture, we will prove them to be reliable. Recently our adult son, John, who designs bridges, called and warmed his mother's heart:

"The proverbs really do work, Mom."

"What do you mean?"

"I've been designing this bridge in the South where the contractor is really a hothead. We had a conference call yesterday with his firm, and he kept blowing up at me. Each time, I bit my tongue and replied with a soft word."

I smiled. When John was growing up, he had a temper. I knew it could bring destruction to him and his relationships. I also knew that Christ would mellow him, and that His Word could break the chains of escalating wrath. One of the proverbs we often acted out was "A soft word turns away wrath" (15:1).

"Well, did it turn away his wrath?"

"Not at first—but by the third time it did. And then his boss called my firm and raved about my professionalism. My boss assigned me to design another bridge for them!"

The truth can set us free. In contrast, ignoring the truth of Scripture can destroy us. It is interesting that in both Hosea and John the words about clinging to the truth of Scripture, of Jesus, are directed to believers.

> *My people are destroyed for lack of knowledge.*
> —HOSEA 4:6

> *If you abide in My word, you are My disciples indeed. And you shall know the truth, and the truth shall make you free.*
> —JOHN 8:31–32

We may not realize, even though we know the Lord, how saturated in secularity we are. We are often so eager to justify living for ourselves that we shut our eyes to the whole counsel of the Word of God. We want to say we are obeying Scripture, when really, our own desires are directing us.

> A big house, a beautiful car, and lots of money: so many have it. Shouldn't I have the same? I mean, I'm a child of the King. He promised me abundant life and said I can have everything in Him.

> Why shouldn't I be happy? I know that God wants obedience, but in this area it's just too hard, and I think God wants His child to enjoy life.

> Isn't God a God of love? Isn't that the most important thing on earth? As long as there is love, how could anything be wrong?

> The absolute truths of God make me look a little bit too intolerant. After all, didn't Jesus say He came to bring peace?

A single scripture could justify each of these, but it is vital that we keep Scripture in context and see what God is really saying. The whole counsel of the Word of God disagrees with each of these philosophies. Following them, we end up bowing to two Cs: comfort and convenience. Our knees should hit the floor to no other one but Christ. We so often make life more about us and less about Him. What we forget is that the truth is our friend, and the truth can, indeed, set us free.

(*Kathy*) This is so profound for me: the truth is our friend. As I grow with Jesus, I am made more aware of my humanity. No matter how close I get to Him, or how often I pray, I wrestle with my flesh and blood. I really have come to identify more with Paul, when he said, "I am the worst of sinners" (1 Timothy 1:15). I've come to understand that the closer you get to the light, the more the light reveals. So I wrestle and will continue to wrestle with my propensity to sin.

What comes so naturally to us is so unnatural to God. This is because He is supernatural. How I yearn to live with that mind-set as I still have my feet planted on this earth. God's words, some of the things that He has required, I have not always been excited about. My tendency is to want to bend, twist, and turn them in ways that make me comfortable. It takes a lot of going through life to surrender to the fact that He knows best.

Our goal should not be the pursuit of happiness but the pursuit of Jesus. It's amazing how I find a much deeper peace and a contentment knowing that I am under His gaze, and He is pleased. I'm learning slowly but surely that His truths and the Truth, Jesus, are my friends. I find myself having far fewer days where I'm butting heads with the things He has told me to do or the foundations of absolutes He has told me to build my life upon. I trust Him. In a time when people are doing "what's good for them," or what "makes them happy," I yearn to do what's good in His eyes and live in ways that make Him happy.

I AM THE LIFE

When Jesus talked about being the Life, He not only meant heaven, for our eternal life has begun right here, right now. When we think of how we were living our lives before Jesus, looking for love in all the wrong places, we are so thankful to Him. How amazing that He was right there, but we couldn't see Him. We were scurrying around, like the author of Ecclesiastes, trying to find meaning, but we weren't plugged into the Source of life, we weren't grafted into the Vine.

But it is so easy to go back to looking for love in all the wrong places—to stop abiding in the Vine and therefore to droop like a flower cut off. We become confused, unhappy, and anxious again. How Hosea longed for God's people to stay close, to embrace only Him! How John warned believers to abide! We love the portrait preceding this chapter by Martin French. In John, Jesus said, "I am the . . . vine" (15:1). In Hosea He said, "I am like a green pine tree" (14:8 NIV). He is the source of life, and Jesus offers this life to us every day. We have everything we need in Him to live an abundant life. Oh how we often miss the blessings of His riches!

(*Dee*) Whenever I hear God call His people "Ephraim," as He did so often in Hosea, my mind goes to the little village where I spent summers as a child, and to which I still go every summer: Ephraim, Wisconsin. It is a vacation spot, often called "the Cape Cod of the Midwest," on the "thumb" of Wisconsin that juts out into the blue waters of Lake Michigan. As a little girl, I remember asking why the village was named Ephraim. These were the answers I heard:

> "It's in the Bible—and it was religious people who settled here."

> "I think it is in Hosea—something about green pine trees."

> "It means fruitful, I think—and there are all these cherry orchards."

As a teenager, I remember seeing this verse monogrammed on our neighbor's martini glasses:

The drunkards of Ephraim.

—Isaiah 28:1

I was confused. Why was this lovely spot named Ephraim? As an adult I learned that the word in the Bible was a name both for God's people and for fruitfulness. God longs for His people to be fruitful. I also learned that the little Wisconsin resort town was named by Moravians who were fleeing persecution, and when they saw that beautiful spot covered with cherry orchards and pine trees, they named it Ephraim and prayed their lives would be as fruitful as the land.

The closing of Hosea is a summary reminding "Ephraim" of her heritage, predicting her future discipline, but also, her future hope. God remembered how beloved Ephraim, or His people, were to Him:

> *I taught Ephraim to walk,*
> *Taking them by their arms.*

—Hosea 11:3

But even though God loved and had nurtured Ephraim, they were

bent on backsliding.

—Hosea 11:7

When God realized He had to discipline His people strongly, His heart was torn:

How can I give you up, Ephraim?

—HOSEA 11:8

The anguish and tenderness in Hosea 11 is that of a Father who dearly loves His child. He taught that child to walk, He saw her through the toddler years and cherished her. If only we would realize God always has our best interests at heart.

(*Kathy*) This fatherly picture reminds me of a hectic day when I was driving around town in an effort to accomplish endless things. I stopped for a traffic light, and a little girl and her dad walked across the street in front of my car. She wore bright red overalls, and her black silky hair flowed down her back. Her small white sneakers kept pace with her father's strides. I smiled when I saw her tiny hand wrapped tightly around one of her father's fingers; I remembered doing the same with my father.

In that moment, I longed to be a child again. I drove on, thinking about my current frenzy to get things done: a woman on the go but still God's child. A sense of well-being came over me. And I wrapped my hand around God's finger. He sees what frazzles, frightens, and frustrates me. I took a deep breath as I remembered who I belonged to.

In Hosea, God gave the prophet hope for His people through a vision of a day when they would finally come home, repentant, into their Father's embrace. This beautiful passage closes the book of Hosea.

Ephraim shall say, "What have I to do anymore with idols?"

—HOSEA 14:8

And in response, God said,

I will answer him and care for him.
I am like a green pine tree;
your fruitfulness comes from me.

—HOSEA 14:8 NIV

HE IS THE WAY, HE IS THE TRUTH, AND HE IS THE LIFE

(Kathy) After twenty-five years of relationship with Jesus, I am still amazed when I experience the tender hovering of His Spirit over me. Music is one of the ways I experience this. Just like you, I have a handful of singers who do something deep in my soul. CeCe Winans is one of them. There's a famous quote from the movie *Chariots of Fire:* "When I run I feel His pleasure." I can honestly say that every time I've heard CeCe sing, I can sense His delight in her. How well she is able to truly forget about all that's around her and simply worship the Lord.

At a recent event where both of us were ministering, CeCe took the stage. I was prepared to have a sweet time of basking in the presence of God. As she sang through the first verse of the second song, gratitude for all that God is came over me. I started to weep quietly, thanking the Lord for His love and provision for me. Before I knew it, I fell to my knees and then bowed my head to the floor, heaving uncontrollably. He was there. He was tender. And He was receiving my adoration.

As I continued in worship, CeCe began to sing "Alabaster Box," a song that tells about the sinful woman who was so thankful to Jesus that she poured her most precious possession, her valuable fragrance from an alabaster box, on His feet. I placed my palms on the floor in front of me, as if I were touching His feet. How great was His cost in rescuing me, but also in continuing to deliver me. The floor beneath me was soaked with my tears.

In moments like these, it's easy for people around me to suspect something is desperately wrong, but at that moment, everything was so right. He was hovering sweetly, wooing me once again with His love. He is the Way, the Truth, and the Life. I am so thankful.

FOREVER IN LOVE

We have intently beheld the portraits of Jesus from John and Hosea with you. We've stared and studied, pondered and prayed, and come out in awe of a God who is terrible yet wonderful. We all know that this life will continue to offer disappointments and deep sorrow. But whatever state of heart we find ourselves in, we can believe in the One who has professed to be all we need. He is the One we can count on. He is the One we can cling to. He truly is the Great I AM.

He's so close. Stay near to His heart. He will never leave you. As He holds you through this life, the pain will pass, the tears will no longer flow, and death will be no more. What a wonderful place to be: forever in love with Jesus.

Notes

CHAPTER 1

1. C. S. Lewis, *The Lion, the Witch, and the Wardrobe* (New York: HarperCollins, 2000), 99.
2. R. C. Sproul, *The Holiness of God* (Wheaton, Ill.: Tyndale, 1985), 43, 30, 53, emphasis added.
3. John Piper, *The Pleasures of God* (Sisters, Ore.: Multnomah Publishers, 2000), 20.

CHAPTER 2

1. Dr. Darrell L. Bock, *Jesus According to Scripture* (Grand Rapids: Baker Academic, 2002), 413.
2. Ibid., 408. "Christology" may be defined as the theological study of the person, nature, and role of Christ.
3. W. Hall Harris, "John," in Darrell L. Bock and Eugene Merrill, *The Bible Knowledge Key Word Study: The Gospels* (Colorado Springs: Cook Communication Ministries, 2002), 261.
4. Some of your Bibles may say that this incident was not in the earliest manuscripts of the Scriptures. Darrell Bock explains that what is debated is *when* it occurred, and some say it should be placed in one of the synoptic (Matthew, Mark, Luke) Gospels. However, the evidence that it *did* occur is substantial.
5. R. C. Sproul, "Before Abraham Was, I AM," *Knowing Christ,* Cassette 6 (Orlando: Ligonier Ministries, 1999).

6. "Falling in Love with You," words by Ron Downey © 1982. Used by permission.

CHAPTER 3

1. Bock and Merrill, *Bible Knowledge,* 261.
2. E. Stanley Jones, *The Word Became Flesh* (New York: Abingdon, 1963), 2.
3. Bock, *Jesus,* 411–412.
4. Daniel Wallace, *Greek Grammar Beyond the Basics: An Exegetical Syntax of the New Testament* (Grand Rapids: Zondervan, 1996), 267–269.
5. Bock, Jesus, 411–412.
6. Ibid., 410.

CHAPTER 4

1. Charles Spurgeon, "The Spirit's Work in the New Creation" in *Spurgeon's Expository Encyclopedia,* vol. 9 (Grand Rapids: Baker Books), 117–122.
2. Some argue that portraying Jesus is a violation of the second commandment to "not make an idol." We agree it is a violation to *worship* a representation of Jesus, for then that art *becomes* an idol, but we do not agree that enjoying art in itself is idolatry. Yet it is a good reminder to realize that whether Jesus is portrayed in a movie, a painting, a sculpture, or with a word picture in a book, that these representations can be only shadows. How clear that will be when we see Him face to face!
3. "Hold Me While I Sleep," words by Kathy Troccoli and Delilah Rene © 2000 Sony/ATV Tree Publishing/BMI/Used by permission.
4. "Goodbye For Now," words by Kathy Troccoli © 1998 Sony ATV Tree Publishing/BMI/Used by permission.
5. "A Baby's Prayer," words by Kathy Troccoli © 1997 Sony/ATV Tree Publishing/BMI/Used by permission.
6. Introduction to Hosea, Compton's Interactive Bible CD-ROM, SoftKey Multimedia, 1994, 1995, 1996.
7. James Montgomery Boice, *The Minor Prophets: I. Hosea–Jonah* (Grand Rapids, Baker Books, 1983), 17.
8. E. K. Bailey, "My Name Is Hosea" (message delivered at Moody Bible Institute's Founder's Week, 2000).
9. Compton's Interactive Bible.
10. "I Hope In Your Word," words by Harlan Rogers © Integrity's Hosanna! Music/ASCAP.

CHAPTER 5

1. Derek Kidner, *The Message of Hosea* (Leicester, England: Inter-Varsity Press, 1981), 33.

2. "Mr. Tenderness," words by Kathy Troccoli © 1997 Sony/ATV Tree Publishing/BMI/Used by permission.

3. Max Lucado, *When Christ Comes* (Nashville: Word, 1999), 144.

4. Charles Spurgeon, "The Bride and Her Ornaments: The Sin of Forgetting God," CD-ROM, *The Charles H. Spurgeon Collection,* Ages Software, 1998–2001.

5. R. C. Sproul, "Hosea 1" (Orlando: Cassette Ministry of Ligonier Ministries, 2000).

6. Kidner, *Message,* 27.

7. Ibid.

8. Ibid., 26.

9. Carl Claudy, *Introduction to Freemasonry* (Washington, D.C.: The Temple Publishers, 1931), 38.

10. Albert Pike, *Morals and Dogma: Ancient and Accepted Scottish Rite of Freemasonry* (Richmond, Va.: Edition Book, 1871, reprinted 1947), 524.

11. Masonic Edition of the Holy Bible, under the heading "Light" (Chicago: Consolidated Book Publishers, 1963).

12. Bock and Merrill, *Bible Knowledge,* 283.

13. Adam Clarke, *Clarke's Commentary,* vol. 5. (Nashville: Abingdon, 1977), 535.

14. John Calvin, *Calvin's Commentaries,* vol. 20 (Grand Rapids: Baker Books, reprinted 1999), 340.

15. Sproul, "Hosea 1."

CHAPTER 6

1. Mike Mason, *The Mystery of Marriage* (Portland, Ore.: Multnomah Press, 1985), 11–13.

2. Dee Brestin, *The Friendships of Women* (Colorado Springs: Cook, 1985), 62–63.

3. "Standing in the Gap," words by Babbie Mason © May Sun Publishing/Word Music LLC/Warner Chappell Music Inc/BMI/Used by permission.

4. Charles Spurgeon, "Strange Ways of Love," CD-ROM, *The Charles H. Spurgeon Collection,* Ages Software, 1998–2001.

5. Kidner, *Message,* 34.

6. Charles Spurgeon, "God's Work in Man," CD-ROM, *The Charles H. Spurgeon Collection*, Ages Software, 1998–2001.

7. Sproul, "Hosea 1."

CHAPTER 7

1. "Live For the Lord," words by Kathy Troccoli © 2000 Sony/ATV Tree Publishing/BMI/Used by permission.

2. Mason, *The Gospel According to Job* (Wheaton: Crossway, 1994), 215.

3. Ibid., 216.

4. Ibid., 215–216.

5. Ibid.

6. Jill has become Dee's office manager and accompanies Dee and Kathy to their combined speaking events.

7. Walter Wangerin, *The Book of God: The Bible as a Novel* (Grand Rapids: Zondervan, 1996), 320–322.

8. Kidner, *Message,* 31.

9. Boice, *Minor Prophets,* 36.

10. Bock and Merrill, *Bible Knowledge,* 268–269.

11. C. S. Lewis, *Prince Caspian* (New York: HarperCollins, 1951), 150.

12. Calvin, *Commentaries,* vol. 19, 226.

CHAPTER 8

1. Leon Morris, *The New International Commentary on the New Testament: The Gospel According to John* (Grand Rapids: Wm. B. Eerdmans Publishing Co., 1971), 194.

2. H. D. M. Spence, *The Pulpit Commentary,* vol. 17 (Peabody, Mass.: John Hendrickson, 1985) 87.

3. Darrell Bock explains, "What John has placed early in his Gospel, all other Gospels place in the last week of Jesus' career. Many simply argue that there was only one cleansing, almost ruling on the matter before considering the option of two cleansings. The accounts' differences do merit consideration that two cleansings are intended." Bock, *Jesus,* 426.

4. John White, *The Golden Cow* (Downers Grove, Ill.: InterVarsity Press, 1979), 7.

5. Boice, *Minor Prophets,* 57.

6. Ian Tait as quoted by Bryan Chapell, *Christ-Centered Preaching,* (Grand Rapids: Baker Books, 1994), 17.

7. Boice, *Minor Prophets,* 53.

8. Kidner, *Message,* 106.

9. Lewis, *The Lion,* 99.

CHAPTER 9
1. R. C. Sproul, "The Way, The Truth, and The Life," Tape 4 from *Knowing Christ: The I AM Sayings of Jesus* (Orlando: Ligonier Ministries, 2002).
2. Ibid.
3. "Who Am I," words by Christy and Nathaniel Nockels © Rocketown Music LLC/Sweater Weather Music/Word Music LLC/Warner Chappell Music Inc/BMI/Used by permission.
4. Bill Maher, interview by Larry King, *Larry King Live,* CNN, December 17, 2003.
5. Dallas Willard, *The Divine Conspiracy* (San Francisco: HarperSanFrancisco, 1998), x.